GW00702796

DARWINISM

TODAY

WARRIOR LOVERS

EROTIC FICTION, EVOLUTION AND FEMALE SEXUALITY

Catherine Salmon and Donald Symons

Weidenfeld & Nicolson
LONDON

First published in Great Britain in 2001
by Weidenfeld & Nicolson

A CIP catalogue record for this book is available
from the British Library.

ISBN 0 297 64701 6

Typeset by Deltatype Ltd, Birkenhead, Merseyside
Printed by Clays Ltd, St Ives plc

Weidenfeld & Nicolson

The Orion Publishing Group Ltd
Orion House
5 Upper Saint Martin's Lane
London, WC2H 9EA

CONTENTS

••

FOREWORD

Darwinism Today is a series of short books by leading figures in the field of evolutionary theory. Each title is an authoritative pocket introduction to the Darwinian ideas that are setting today's intellectual agenda.

The series developed out of the Darwin@LSE programme at the London School of Economics, where the Darwin Seminars provide a platform for distinguished evolutionists to present the latest Darwinian thinking and to explore its application to humans. The programme is having an enormous impact, both in helping to popularize evolutionary theory and in fostering cross-disciplinary approaches to shared problems.

With the publication of **Darwinism Today** we hope that the best of the new Darwinian ideas will reach an even wider audience.

Helena Cronin and Oliver Curry

WARRIOR LOVERS

LOVERS

EROTIC FICTION, EVOLUTION
AND FEMALE SEXUALITY

PROLOGUE

••

One day in the spring of 1994 I received an e-mail message that left me so dumbstruck that I had to re-read it very slowly to make sure that it actually said what it had seemed to say. The message was from Catherine Salmon, whom I had never met, a doctoral candidate in evolutionary psychology at McMaster University in Hamilton, Ontario, and a student of my old friends Martin Daly and Margo Wilson. Catherine explained that each student in her programme was required to complete seven empirical research projects on the road to the Ph.D., each under the supervision of a different professor (who did not have to be at McMaster). She was writing to ask whether I would be willing to supervise research on something called 'slash fiction', which, she explained, is a kind of romance fiction – often very sexually graphic – written by and for women, in which both lovers are men. To be considered 'true' slash, the protagonists must be an expropriated media pairing, such as Captain Kirk/Mr Spock from the original *Star Trek* series, or Sherlock Holmes/Dr Watson, the word 'slash' referring to the punctuation mark between the men's names.

What perplexed and intrigued me about Catherine's message was not so much that I had never heard of slash (after all, the world is full of things I've never heard of), but that I could not imagine why any woman would want to read or write such fiction. This was embarrassing, because the reason that Catherine had sought me out as a potential supervisor was that I had written extensively on the evolution of human sexual psychology – which, of course, included women's sexual psychology. In 1979 I had published *The Evolution of Human Sexuality*, a central theme of which is that 'with respect to sexuality, there is a female human nature and a male human nature, and these natures are extraordinarily different . . . because throughout the immensely long hunting and gathering phase of human evolutionary history the sexual desires and dispositions that were adaptive for either sex were for the other tickets to reproductive oblivion' (from the Preface). Even more relevant to slash fiction was a 1990 article that psychologist Bruce Ellis and I had published in the *Journal of Sex Research*, in which we had reported the results of our empirical research on men's and women's sexual fantasies. In discussing the implications of our findings, we had noted that the striking differences between the fantasies of our male and female subjects were echoed by the differences between male-oriented and female-oriented commercial eroticas: that is, between pornography and romance novels. While working on that article I had forced myself to read a few romance novels, in addition to the academic literature on that topic, yet none of my readings had prepared me for the existence of slash.

After digesting Catherine's e-mail message, I concluded that there must be more in women's mating psychology than had been dreamt of in my philosophy. I immediately agreed to help with her research, hoping thereby to discover what aspects of female sexuality had managed to stay under my radar for all those years and to determine whether slash could shed any light on the selection pressures that operated on our female ancestors.

In due course, a large package from Catherine arrived in my office containing a diverse sampling of slash fiction as well as a few male/male romances in which the lovers were not an expropriated media pair. My reactions to these narratives were mixed. Considered strictly as fiction, I found them pretty tedious (although some were very well written). Considered as clues to women's mating psychology, however, I found them riveting.

In some respects, slash turned out to be less peculiar than I had assumed it would be, based on Catherine's brief description and on her warning about lengthy and graphic male/male sex scenes. In fact, slash seemed oddly familiar, and it dawned on me that these narratives were in many ways like the mainstream romances that I had read just a few years earlier.

My reactions to reading romance novels and slash fiction may be a bit reminiscent of the reactions that many women have when viewing porn videos, especially for the first time (Good grief, are men actually turned on by this? Can this possibly be what men really want?). To encounter erotica designed to appeal to the other sex is to gaze into the psychological abyss that separates the sexes and, what's worse, to confront one's own short-comings *vis-à-vis* the other sex's fantasy ideal. The contrasts between romance novels and porn videos are so numerous and profound that they can make one marvel that men and women ever get together at all, much less stay together and successfully rear children.

In the months that followed, Catherine and I engaged in an intensive e-mail dialogue (much longer than this book), which led to rapid advances in my slash education and to our working out a few basic questions that we hoped to be able to answer in a short-term, low-budget empirical study. Early in our correspondence, Catherine revealed that her interest in slash was more than academic. She 'came out' to me as a long-time slash fan, an active member of the slash community (as both a reader and a writer), a regular contributor to on-line discussions about slash, and a master of the academic literature on slash. Most slash fans, including Catherine, are intensely curious about the nature of slash, and they speculate endlessly about the sources of its unique appeal. Some of the most productive questions that we eventually asked our research subjects were derived not from evolutionary theory, but from Catherine's keen and subtle intuition, which had been honed during her many years in the slash community.

What I brought to the partnership was a fresh eye, a male perspective and a long history of reading and writing about the evolution of human sexuality. Also, because the existence of slash fiction was the first really startling fact about human sexuality I'd come across in a long time, I was almost obsessively interested in getting to the bottom of it (so to speak). Although I undoubtedly profited more than Catherine did from our e-mail correspondence, I think she learned a few things as well. For example, at one point she floated the idea that although slash fandom is an almost exclusively female domain, gay men might also enjoy reading slash. I replied that, in light of the many similarities between slash and mainstream romances, it seemed to me unlikely that slash would find a receptive audience among gay or any other kind of men. I suggested that she try out a few sexually graphic examples of slash on gay men, which she proceeded to do. Reading between the lines of her next e-mail message, I sensed that she had been a little shocked when these men had laughed (politely, of course) at the slash. And I think she was also taken aback when, at her request, they showed her a few examples of the kind of erotica that actually did turn them on. She especially noted the absence of character development and plot in gay male porn.

The key question that Catherine and I hoped to make some headway with was: why does slash exist at all? Similarities between slash and boy/girl romances not-withstanding, the majority of slash fans not only prefer slash, but infrequently read mainstream romances. Our goal was to unearth the source of slash's unique appeal to its fans.

What distinguishes slash fans from the tens of millions of women who read mainstream romances (and have probably never heard of slash) might conceivably be some sort of psychosexual quirk among the former – analogous, say, to male paraphiliacs (aka fetishists) who can be sexually aroused only by women's shoes or only by rubber clothing. We decided to test this hypothesis by determining whether ordinary women readers of mainstream romances would also enjoy a male/male romance. If they didn't, that might lend support to the 'psychosexual quirk' hypothesis; but if they did, that would count against this hypothesis. Our experiment and its results are described in Chapter 7. In Chapter 8 we present our current thinking on the question: why does slash exist?

Donald Symons

CHAPTER 1

••

Introduction

'You, Spock, at Jim Kirk's side: it's as if you have always been there and always will.'

Edith, a 1930s woman in love with Kirk, replying to Spock's question of where she thought he and Kirk belonged ('City on the Edge of Forever', *Star Trek* episode by Harlan Ellison)

In this book we present a Darwinian analysis of slash fiction. To many readers this probably makes about as much sense as a Newtonian analysis of hip-hop music. So we would like to begin by explaining what we do and do not mean.

We emphatically do *not* mean that humans evolved adaptations to read and write slash fiction. Slash has existed since the 1970s; fiction has existed for perhaps 2500 years; writing has existed for only about 5000 years and, until recently, only a small portion of humanity was literate. Neither slash, nor fiction, nor writing itself has existed long enough for humans to have adapted to it via the glacially slow process that Charles Darwin discovered: natural selection.

Nor do we mean that by reading and writing slash fiction the fans of this genre are in some obscure way promoting their own reproduction and thereby ensuring the survival of their genes.

What we *do* mean is this. Slash exists because a sizeable international community of women derives pleasure from creating and consuming it. The essential features of this genre thus contain information about human female psychological adaptations, which, like all adaptations in all species, are the products of evolution by natural selection. Identifying the essential features of slash fiction, comparing these features with those of mainstream women's erotica, and contrasting women's and men's eroticas is one way to illuminate evolved female mating psychology.

Our combined thirty-five years of experience teaching the basic concepts of organic evolution and evolutionary psychology to university students, as well as writing on these and related topics for both general professional and lay audiences, have convinced us that few people are well informed about these matters and that most people, alas, have been systematically misinformed – and thus are hampered by a host of misconceptions. For example, most educated people seem to believe at least some of the following: that natural selection favours the 'survival of the species'; that beneath the conflict and competition that characterize the interactions of living things an underlying unity and harmony prevails; that evolutionary explanations are tautologies or just-so stories (fables rather than scientific accounts of how species acquired particular traits); that genes are usefully conceptualized as conscious entities that manipulate us for their own ends; that knowledge of the past is inherently conjectural because the past cannot be observed 'directly'; that there is a significant theoretical difference between the evolution of psychological (brain) mechanisms and the evolution of other kinds of biological mechanism; that there exist coherent theories of human action that do *not* assume a universal human nature; that the human brain comprises only a few general-purpose mechanisms (such as 'being smart' or 'having a capacity for culture'); that human male and female psychologies differ only in trivial ways, if at all. These notions are not just wrong, they are so profoundly wrong that believing them to be true – or, what is worse, implicitly assuming them to be true – makes it virtually impossible to appreciate the power of Darwinism to illuminate human affairs.

A Darwinian analysis of slash fiction cannot be understood apart from the scientific framework in which it is embedded. The study of women's mating psychology is a sub-field of human mating psychology, which is a sub-field of evolutionary psychology, which itself is a sub-field of the adaptationist programme. Our aim in the first part of this book is to establish the requisite scientific framework, starting with a description of the adaptationist programme. In the later chapters we discuss the nature and significance of slash.

CHAPTER 2

••

The Adaptationist
Programme in Biology

It has always been intuitively obvious, even to children, that living things consist of many integrated parts, each with a distinct function or purpose. To say that something has a function is to say that it was designed to solve a particular problem. The function of a claw hammer is to drive and to pull nails; the function of the heart is to pump blood (that is, the heart solves the problem of circulating blood); the function of leaves is to provide energy via photosynthesis; the function of islet cells in the pancreas is to produce insulin, which, in turn, functions to enable the body's cells to absorb glucose. And on and on. At every level of biological inquiry – molecular, cell, tissue, organ, organ system and whole organism – living things exhibit an exquisitely intricate *functional* organization that non-living things, other than human artefacts, completely lack. The problem-solving devices that make up living organisms are called 'adaptations', and the goal of the adaptationist programme in biology is to identify and describe these adaptations, to partition organisms 'naturally' into their functional components. In short, unlike physics or chemistry or astronomy or geology, the core of the biological sciences is the study of *functional* organization.

Such a programme has existed for centuries. For example, William Harvey's discovery almost 300 years ago that the function of the heart is to pump blood was a major contribution to the adaptationist programme. But until 1859, when Charles Darwin published *On the Origin of Species by Means of Natural Selection*, no natural process had been discovered that was capable of creating and maintaining adaptations.

Darwin observed that plant and animal breeders systematically modify species over the course of generations by capitalizing on two indisputable facts: first, the individuals that make up each species vary in most of their characteristics; second, offspring tend to resemble their parents more than they resemble other members of their species. By practising selective breeding – that is, by allowing only those individuals with desired characteristics to reproduce – humans transformed a wolf into a chihuahua in the blink of an eye, as reckoned on a geological timescale.

Darwin proposed that a process analogous to selective breeding occurs in nature, but in nature no external entity or agent does the 'selecting'. Rather, there is simply random variation in the hereditary material (mutation) coupled with systematic *non*-random replication of the variants. Those individuals who are better adapted to their environments produce more surviving offspring, on average, than do less well-adapted individuals, and their offspring inherit their parents' superior adaptations. Iterated over long periods of time, this process, which is called 'natural selection', results in the evolution of species. If Darwin's theory of adaptation through natural selection is correct, every adaptation in every species exists because it promoted the reproduction of individuals in ancestral populations more effectively than did the available alternatives. In this sense, every adaptation can be said to be a reproductive adaptation.

In Darwin's day, essentially nothing was known about the physical bases of heredity. Darwin observed the existence of heritable variation in plant and animal populations, and he incorporated it into his theory; but he could not explain it. Although Gregor Mendel discovered in the 1860s that the development of organisms is controlled by discrete particles – now called genes – that are passed from one generation to the next, his research was unknown to the scientific community during the nineteenth century, and the discovery that genes are DNA molecules lay almost a century in the future. A modern restatement of Darwin's theory is the following: over the course of generations, an adaptation causes its own spread throughout a population because it more effectively promotes the replication of the genes that directed its construction than do the available alternatives.

Pursuing the adaptationist programme

An organism can be partitioned into 'traits' in an infinite number of ways, and the overwhelming majority of arbitrarily demarcated traits are not adaptations but, rather, by-products of adaptations. To propose that a trait is an adaptation is not merely to propose that it evolved from something else (every trait has an evolutionary history), but rather to propose that the trait *per se* was designed by natural selection to perform some function. The whiteness of bone, for example, is not in itself an adaptation because whiteness *per se* has no function. Bone was designed by natural selection for its structural properties, not for its colour. Whiteness is merely an incidental by-product.

To identify and describe an adaptation, it is not necessary to know the specific genes that control the adaptation's development; nor is it necessary to have a fossil record of the adaptation. William Harvey knew nothing of the genes that control the development of hearts (the discovery of genes lay far in the future), and there were no fossil hearts available for study; but that did not prevent him from demonstrating that the heart is an adaptation whose function is to pump blood.

The adaptationist programme is pursued in two complementary ways. The first is the approach Harvey used, a sort of 'engineering' analysis, in which the scientist attempts to discern a functional fit – like a lock and key – between an adaptive problem faced by individuals in ancestral populations and specific properties of the organism that are so well-engineered to solve that problem that they cannot be the product of chance. For example, the complexity, precision, efficiency, multiplicity and integration of the many parts that collectively make up the eye constitute overwhelming engineering evidence for the eye's functional role in vision.

The second way to discover and describe adaptations is the comparative method, wherein a series of living species is compared with respect to some trait. Here is an example of how this method works. Although the function of testes in male mammals is obvious, the functional significance of the *size* of the testes in any given species is not. In fact, if there were only one species of mammal in the world, it would be difficult to draw any functional conclusions about testes size. But when the testes-to-body ratio is compared across an array of mammalian species, a dramatic pattern emerges. This ratio turns out to be strongly correlated with species' breeding systems. In species like the common chimpanzee, where females often mate with many males during a single fertile period, the male who deposits the most sperm in the female's reproductive tract is most likely to impregnate her, just as the person who buys the most lottery tickets is most likely to win the lottery. In such species, natural selection tends to favour the evolution of relatively large testes (a high testes-to-body ratio), because the larger the testes, the greater the sperm volume in each ejaculate. By contrast, in species like the gorilla, where females normally mate with only one male during each fertile period – and, hence, the male's sperm do not compete with the sperm of other males to fertilize the egg – natural selection tends to favour relatively small testes (selection penalizes waste, so testes are no larger than they need to be). The fact that this ratio in humans is intermediate between chimpanzees and gorillas constitutes evidence that, during the course of human evolutionary history, sperm competition was typically less intense among ancestral human males than among chimpanzees but more intense than among gorillas.

Studies of the fossil record, of the archaeological record, of living hunter-gatherer peoples and of how genes control the development of bodies can be highly informative and can inspire hypotheses about adaptations; but none is a *necessary* ingredient of the adaptationist programme.

The environment of evolutionary adaptedness

It is logically impossible to describe an adaptation, in functional terms, without at least implicitly describing the specific features of the environment to which the adaptation is adapted. For example, one could not possibly describe the adaptations that constitute the visual system without implying the existence of such features of the environment as electromagnetic radiation of certain frequencies, stable objects with edges, fluctuating levels of illumination, object motion in space, and so forth. Furthermore, since natural selection is the only process capable of producing adaptations, every description of an adaptation necessarily includes specific assumptions or hypotheses about relatively stable features of *past* environments. For example, the hypothesis that specialized edge-detecting cells exist in mammalian brains necessarily implies the assumption that objects with edges were persistent features of visual environments in ancestral populations. Each adaptation thus can be said to have its own 'environment of evolutionary adaptedness'.

Many scientists assume, incorrectly, that this environment refers to a particular time and place – so, for example, the 'human environment of evolutionary adaptedness' is often thought to be the African savanna during the Stone Age. But it is really individual adaptations rather than species that have such environments. Some human adaptations did indeed evolve during the last few million years on the savannas of Africa, but others (such as the four-chambered heart) evolved many millions of years earlier. In short, the environment of evolutionary adaptedness refers not to a particular time and place, but to the specific features of ancestral environments to which an adaptation is adapted and upon which its normal development and functioning depend.

If components of an adaptation's evolutionary environment are absent or altered, the adaptation may not develop or function normally. For example, our visual system contains adaptations whose function is to maintain 'colour constancy', so that we perceive an object as having a constant colour even though the light frequencies reflected from its surface continually fluctuate. If we lacked these colour constancy adaptations, we would perceive objects suddenly changing colour whenever a cloud passed over the sun, and objects would appear to be a different colour at 10 a.m. than they are at noon. Our colour constancy adaptations evolved in environments in which the predominant light source was the sun, so the solar spectrum of electromagnetic radiation is part of their ancestral environment. When the spectrum of a light source differs dramatically from the solar spectrum, our colour constancy mechanisms don't function normally, which is why it can sometimes be hard to recognize your own car in a car park lit by sodium vapour lamps.

As the above examples illustrate, we know many things about the evolutionary past with virtual certainty. We know, for example, that life evolved in, and is adapted to, an earth-strength gravitational field, that objects with edges have always existed in the visual fields of organisms, that the primary light source has always been the sun. We know that, during the course of human evolutionary history, women were pregnant for nine months and nursed their infants, and that men never became pregnant and never nursed.

Four important – but persistently misunderstood – points emerge from the preceding discussion. First, adaptationist hypotheses are scientific, fully capable of being tested. They are not, as is sometimes claimed, untestable just-so stories. If that charge were true, physiology would not be a science, and the hypothesis that the heart is a pump would be mere untestable conjecture, no more credible than the hypothesis that it is an organ of vision or digestion.

Second, the notion of the environment of evolutionary adaptedness is not optional: it is intrinsically embedded in every description of a biological phenomenon in which *function* is stated or implied, whether or not that description explicitly contains such words as 'evolution', 'natural selection', 'ancestral populations' or 'adaptation'. Every description of a physiological process (such as 'the function of islet cells is to secrete insulin') entails definite hypotheses or assumptions about that process's ancestral environment.

Third, hypotheses about this environment are rarely mere speculations or conjectures. We know literally thousands of things about ancient environments with virtual certainty.

Fourth, an adaptation is a kind of time machine – not in the sense that it can transport us to the past, but in the sense that it can transport information about the past to us. Manifested in every complex adaptation's design is a record of millions of selection events, which occurred over the course of thousands or millions of years among millions of individuals in ancestral populations. The existence of adaptations in our tongues designed specifically to detect sugar, for example, tells us that sugar was a persistent feature of ancestral environments, and the fact that sugar is 'sweet' – that it tastes good – provides strong evidence about its nutritional role during the course of our evolutionary history.

CHAPTER 3

●●●

Evolutionary Psychology

Evolutionary psychology is the branch of the adaptationist programme whose goal is to discover and describe the
psychological adaptations that constitute the human
brain. Just as the stomach is the organ of digestion and
the lungs are the organs of respiration, the brain is the
organ of behaviour. Organisms, such as plants, that do
not behave do not have brains. There is no theoretical
difference between psychological adaptations, which are
made of nerve cells, and non-psychological adaptations,
which are made of other kinds of cell; nor is there a
special theory of the evolution of brains or of behaviour.
Human psychological adaptations, like all adaptations in
all species, are the products of ordinary natural selection.

In essence, evolutionary psychology is simply psychological research that is inspired and guided by evolutionary facts and principles. The psychological mechanisms (adaptations) that constitute the human brain are universals in our species. Pathological conditions aside, every human being has the abilities to see and to speak a natural language, to regulate body temperature and blood pressure, to experience joy, fear, nausea, sexual jealousy and many other things.

Every theory of human action, not just evolutionary ones, implies the existence of universal psychological mechanisms. For example, the theory that human action is 'culturally constructed' implies that all human beings possess psychological mechanisms that underpin the process of 'cultural construction', whatever that may entail. If humans have culture while elm trees, lizards and lemurs don't, it must be because humans have certain psychological adaptations that elm trees, lizards and lemurs lack. In short, the *existence* of a universal 'human nature' is not at issue. What *is* at issue is the nature of that nature: that is, the number and kinds of universal psychological adaptations that make up the human brain.

Furthermore, if every theory of human action implies the existence of universal psychological mechanisms, then every theory of human action necessarily implies the existence of some past causal process that produced those mechanisms (nothing comes from nothing) and past environments in which this production occurred. The only known causal process capable of producing and maintaining functional mechanisms is evolution by natural selection. Therefore, every theory of human action necessarily implies the existence of universal psychological mechanisms that were shaped by natural selection in ancestral human populations. When evolutionary psychologists propose hypotheses about human nature that include, as part of their formulation, explicit assumptions or hypotheses about past selection pressures and ancestral environments, they are not being more *speculative* than other students of human behaviour, as is often claimed; they are being more *explicit*.

In an important sense, there is no such thing as 'evolutionary psychology' because there is no such thing as *non*-evolutionary psychology (after all, scientific psychologists cannot be 'creationists'). Evolutionary psychology is likely to be a temporary discipline, which will exist only as long as it is needed. As psychologists of all stripes come to make explicit their currently implicit hypotheses about human nature, past selection pressures and environments of evolutionary adaptedness, evolutionary psychology will wither away as a distinct field and all psychology will be 'evolutionary' – for precisely the same reason that all biology is evolutionary. Psychology is, after all, a branch of biology.

Specialized psychological mechanisms

During the course of human evolutionary history our ancestors were faced with many different kinds of adaptive behavioural problems – finding food, not becoming food, choosing a place to live, forming coalitions, selecting mates, caring for children and many, many more. Different kinds of problems require different kinds of adaptation to solve them. The human female body, for example, contains *both* a womb *and* a heart, rather than some dual- or multi-purpose organ, because the design features that make an organ effective at protecting and nourishing an embryo and foetus are different from and incompatible with the design features that make an organ effective at pumping blood. Similarly, the human brain must comprise a very large number of psychological mechanisms and sub-mechanisms that are specialized for solving diverse problems in different domains. The psychological mechanisms underpinning food choice must differ from those underpinning mate choice because the criteria that reliably determined 'nutritional value' over evolutionary time were utterly different from those that determined 'mate value'. For example, bilateral (left/right) symmetry was a desirable feature in a potential mate, because it was a reliable indicator of good health, good genes and other aspects of mate value; but it was an irrelevant feature in a potential meal, because it predicted nothing about nutritional value. So, to incorporate a bilateral symmetry 'detector and assessor' into mate selection psychology would have been highly adaptive, whereas it would have been highly maladaptive to incorporate such an adaptation into food selection psychology.

It is sometimes proposed that our Stone Age ancestors could have solved all the adaptive behavioural problems they faced by evolving a single general-purpose psychological mechanism, such as 'being smart' or 'figuring things out'; but such proposals are mere hand-waving. To be taken seriously, they would need to include a description of the actual design features of such a miraculous mechanism: that is, how, exactly, does *any* entity – human, nonhuman animal or inanimate machine – 'be smart'? When this question is taken seriously, the answer invariably turns out to be that 'smartness' is achieved by integrating a large number of special-purpose devices, each of which instantiates in its design a great deal of information that enables it to perform one kind of task well. In short, human behaviour is more complex and more variable than that of any other organism because we have more, not fewer, psychological mechanisms than any other organism has, just as a computer is 'smarter' than a toaster because a computer has more specialized parts than a toaster does.

We do not have conscious access to the vast majority of our psychological processes. They work as automatically and unobtrusively as do digestion and blood pressure regulation (when functioning normally). For example, the incredibly complex and sophisticated machinery that underpins our ability to see is not accessible to introspection; nor is there any adaptive reason why it should be. Our ancestors would have derived no adaptive benefit from being able to access the underlying machinery of vision consciously. Neither we nor any other animal with eyes needs to know how this machinery works, or even that it exists, in order to see. All we need to do is to open our eyes.

Misinterpretations of Darwinism

Many writers on human evolution have seriously misled their readers about the implications of Darwinism for the study of human nature and behaviour. One common error is to conceive of humans as 'constrained' by their psychological adaptations (the subtitle of one book on this topic is *Constraints on the Human Spirit*). This is an odd, almost perverse, way of thinking about brain adaptations. These adaptations do not *constrain* us, any more than do the adaptations that underpin digestion or respiration. On the contrary, our brain adaptations *enable* our feelings, thoughts, perceptions, memories and actions. No one would describe the heart or the liver as 'constraining' the pumping or detoxification of blood; the heart and the liver *enable* these processes. In the absence of the many adaptations that constitute our digestive system, we would not suddenly find ourselves unconstrained, able to digest everything; on the contrary, we would find ourselves unable to digest anything. Similarly, in the absence of our psychological adaptations, no disembodied spirit would suddenly emerge, as from a chrysalis, to soar free and unconstrained, to think whatever thoughts it is possible to think and to feel whatever feelings it is possible to feel; on the contrary, there would be no thoughts, no feelings, no mental phenomena, no 'us' at all.

Another common error is to imagine genes, metaphorically, as conscious entities that *want* to survive and that strive to achieve this goal by manipulating us. But genes do not whisper in our mind's ear (as one biologist implied in the title *The Whisperings Within*); nor are they puppet-masters that pull our strings. We are not 'possessed' by our genes. They are not selfish or altruistic, gay or straight, witty or dull. They do not have plans or goals. They are simply DNA molecules that control the development of bodies by controlling the process of protein synthesis.

A similar but somewhat more subtle error is to imagine that humans evolved to *strive*, consciously or unconsciously, to 'maximize' their reproduction and thereby promote the replication of their genes. As discussed earlier, however, there is no such thing as a general problem-solver – including a 'reproduction maximizer' – because there is no such thing as a general problem. Organisms are collections of specialized devices that, over evolutionary time and on the average, promoted – *in some specific way* – the survival of the genes that directed their construction. There are adaptations in the digestive system whose function is to produce bile and there are adaptations in the visual system whose function is to maintain perceptual constancies; but there are no adaptations in the brains of any species whose function is to promote gene survival 'in general'; nor could such an adaptation possibly evolve. There *is* no 'general' way to achieve this goal. In sum, evolutionary psychologists do not assume that humans evolved or could have evolved a conscious or unconscious motive to promote the survival of their genes.

A corollary of the above is that when organisms develop or exist in evolutionarily novel environments, their adaptations will not necessarily promote gene survival efficiently, or, indeed, at all. For example, despite heroic efforts by biologists and zoo personnel, it often proves difficult or impossible to induce certain animal species to breed in the evolutionarily novel conditions of captivity. Similarly, humans evolved a taste for sugar, fat and salt because these substances were both nutritious and relatively difficult to obtain during the overwhelming majority of human evolutionary history. In recent, evolutionarily novel environments, however, in which technology and capitalism have rendered these tasty substances abundant and cheap, most of us consume far more of them than is good for us. Given the options available in the modern world, most of us could make far healthier and more 'adaptive' dietary choices than we do; but our gustatory adaptations − like all our complex adaptations, psychological and non-psychological − are designed to function in the conditions and circumstances of the evolutionary past.

The human environment of evolutionary adaptedness

Human adaptations were shaped by natural selection in environments different in many respects from those that most of us encounter today. It is to stable features of these past environments that our adaptations are adapted.

Evidence about the nature of past environments and selection pressures comes from a number of sources, including ethnographies of living hunter-gatherers, the archaeological record and, most importantly, the designs of the adaptations themselves. These complementary lines of evidence indicate that our ancestors' lives were characterized by the following features. (We focus here on those features of the environment of evolutionary adaptedness that are particularly relevant to understanding the evolution of human sexual psychological adaptations and male–female differences therein.)

For over 99 per cent of human evolutionary history, our ancestors hunted and gathered for a living. By the standards of comparatively recent agricultural and industrialized societies, ancestral hunter-gatherer groups and populations were small (and each individual's potential pool of mates was correspondingly small). States, armies, police forces, socioeconomic classes, judicial and banking systems, contraceptive technology and money did not exist. Local, kin-based foraging groups were typically nomadic for most or all of the year, hence there was little opportunity to accumulate material resources. There was an economic division of labour by sex: men primarily hunted medium and large game; women primarily gathered plant foods. Although husbands typically 'invested' substantially in their wives' children, primarily by provisioning and protecting them, hands-on childcare was overwhelmingly the province of mothers and other female kin. Hands-on warfare, by contrast, was almost exclusively the province of males.

In these 'natural fertility' populations, women typically became pregnant when they reached the age of nubility (that is, when they began to have ovulatory menstrual cycles, usually in their early to mid-teens). Women could not have raised more than one child every three to four years, and children were nursed on demand for several years, which hormonally suppresses the resumption of ovulation and delays the arrival of another child. Women were almost always married by the time they became fertile, and if a woman was widowed or divorced, she soon remarried. Thus, if a man copulated with a fertile woman to whom he was not married, she was very probably another man's wife. Most marriages were monogamous; some were polygynous; and only a tiny fraction were polyandrous.

Tests of genetic paternity among a number of living preliterate peoples, including hunter-gatherers, have shown that the vast majority of children (though of course not all) are sired by their mothers' husbands. In other words, 'social' paternity and genetic paternity are very highly correlated, so that among these peoples it is not necessary to be wise to know your own father; he may not be the man your mother was married to when you were conceived, but that's the way to bet. That marriage and male sexual proprietariness are both universals among living preliterate peoples suggests that social and genetic paternity have been highly correlated for many thousands of years.

During the course of human evolution, almost all fertile women were married and husbands were proprietary of their wives' sexuality; therefore, there would have been little if any scope for men to pursue what has been called a 'cad' or love-'em-and-leave-'em 'reproductive strategy', in which a man deliberately remains single in order to sow his wild oats with many women – whose children he will not invest in – before settling down. On the contrary, an effective male reproductive strategy was to acquire a wife as soon as possible, to acquire additional wives when possible, and to capitalize on sexual opportunities with other men's wives whenever the risks were low enough. In the competition for women, such attributes as good health, vigour, physical and social competence, high status, prowess as hunter or warrior and being a member of a large lineage would have increased a man's chances of marrying young, of obtaining multiple wives and of having low-cost affairs. An effective female reproductive strategy was to choose and be chosen by just such a high-mate-value male, preferably as his only wife. Failing that, women had the choice of being one of the wives of a high-mate-value male, the sole wife of a lower-mate-value male, and of judiciously conducting affairs with married men.

CHAPTER 4

•••

Human Mating Psychology

One adaptive problem that our ancestors regularly faced was mate choice. Potential mates varied in 'mate value' – that is, in the degree to which they would have promoted the reproduction of the individuals who mated with them – just as potential food varied in 'food value' and potential habitats varied in 'habitat value'. For example, eighteen-year-old women would have had higher mate value, on average, than fifty-year-old women. And men who were great hunters would have had higher mate value, on average, than klutzes. Reliable information about an individual's mate value would have been available in specific aspects of his or her physical appearance, behaviour and so forth (for example, skin condition and texture would have provided reliable information about age and many aspects of health).

We should therefore expect natural selection to have produced psychological adaptations specialized to detect and use reliable information about mate value in the context of mate selection. At least that is what most of us would expect if we were considering mate preferences in any animal species other than humans. For example, if we learned that, in a certain bird species, males with the reddest topknots consistently had fewer parasites than other males, and yet the females did *not* show a mating preference for males with the reddest topknots, surely most of us would find this a puzzling fact that needed to be explained. Why, we would wonder, didn't females evolve a preference for the healthiest males, when reliable cues of health were readily and cheaply available?

Nevertheless, most people assume that among humans – and humans alone – the determinants of attractiveness are arbitrary or capricious rather than reliable cues of mate value. This follows from the more general assumption that among humans the perception of attractiveness is completely or largely 'culturally constructed' – which simply means that humans acquire their standards of attractiveness by imitating those of other people. We will argue that the probability of this common assumption being correct is essentially zero.

To understand why, it is important to keep in mind that mating is inherently competitive and that, as far as natural selection is concerned, individuals can be said to be successful or unsuccessful in mating only compared to their competitors. Over evolutionary time, women who chose to mate with a human male would have had more surviving offspring than those who chose to mate with trees or sabre-toothed tigers or other randomly chosen objects in their environment; and women who chose to mate with the village headman would have had more surviving offspring, on average, than those who chose the village idiot. But we should expect the psychological mechanisms underpinning a reproductively significant activity such as mate choice to make much more subtle and refined discriminations than these. Natural selection, like the proverbial mills of God, grinds slowly but exceedingly fine. The evolutionary process that shaped our psychological adaptations, including our mate choice adaptations, is the same process that produced stick insects that are virtually indistinguishable from sticks, the same process that produced rod cells in the retinas of our eyes that are so sensitive they can potentially respond to a single photon of light.

Why attractiveness perception is neither arbitrary nor culturally constructed

Imagine that in ancestral human populations there were ten different observable cues or indices of mate value, each of which tracked at least one component of mate value that was not tracked by any other. In such circumstances, individuals who could detect and use only one cue would have out-reproduced individuals who simply chose their mates at random; but the former would themselves have been out-reproduced by individuals who could detect and use two cues (as long as the costs of detection were not too high). And so on. Individuals who could detect and use all ten cues would have produced more surviving offspring than individuals who could detect and use only nine, over evolutionary time and on average, because they would have been able to make slightly better mating decisions. In sum, in ancestral populations, mate preferences as manifested in subjective experiences of mate 'attractiveness' would have varied directly with mate value. Psychological mechanisms of attractiveness perception that led to largely or completely non-utilitarian, arbitrary, capricious, whimsical, idiosyncratic mate choices could not have been produced by selection, and if such mechanisms had somehow sprung into existence by chance, they would have been eliminated rapidly by selection. For this reason, mate attractiveness cannot be completely or largely 'culturally constructed'.

To better see why this is so, imagine an ancestral human population in which individuals acquired their standards of mate attractiveness in much the same way as they acquired the words in their language: from one another. In human language the relationships between sounds and meanings are arbitrary, and for good reasons. The function of language is communication within a local group of native speakers, hence it makes no functional difference whether a particular large mammal is called a 'mastodon' or a 'heffalump'. All that matters is that everyone in the group understands and uses the same word. (The psychological machinery underpinning this system of language acquisition must be orders of magnitude simpler, cheaper and more flexible than a system in which the relations between sounds and meanings are specified innately.) A by-product of this system of language acquisition is that languages 'drift' with the passage of time, so that ancestor and descendant languages eventually become mutually unintelligible. This was not an adaptive problem in the non-literate human populations in which language evolved, because individuals needed to communicate only with the living, not with their long-dead ancestors.

But what if the perception of mate attractiveness was completely or largely underpinned by a psychological mechanism that instantiated a rule such as: 'Look around and see what traits others perceive as attractive, then be attracted to individuals with those traits'? The determinants of mate attractiveness would drift capriciously with the passages of time, just as languages do, and the relationship between mate attractiveness and mate value would be as arbitrary as that between sound and meaning. For example, in some populations men would perceive wrinkled skin as an attractive feature in a potential mate, in others as unattractive, and in most as having no systematic effect whatever on attractiveness. In such circumstances, any random genetic change (mutation) that caused its bearers to prefer, even slightly, a reliable cue of high mate value in the other sex (such as unwrinkled female skin) would have a strong selective advantage. Therefore, any system in which the criteria of mate attractiveness were completely or largely 'culturally constructed' would soon be replaced by one in which mate attractiveness varied directly with cues of mate value.

Other people's perceptions are likely to play a role in determining attractiveness perception – but only a very limited one. For example, women may perceive a male stranger as more attractive if he has a pretty woman on his arm than if he is alone; and the prettier the woman he is with the more attractive he may appear to be. The adaptationist logic underlying this hypothesis is as follows: the very fact that a man has been chosen by a pretty woman provides low-cost information about non-observable aspects of his mate value, and the prettier the woman who did the choosing the higher his mate value is likely to be. In other words, women observers can acquire information about a man's mate value via a sort of information parasitism. Nevertheless, it is clear that (a) human beings evolved psychological mechanisms for detecting and assessing cues of mate value that are independent of other people's preferences, (b) these mechanisms account for a very large proportion of individual variability in attractiveness, and (c) these mechanisms are highly resistant to 'cultural' modification.

CHAPTER 5

••

Male–Female Differences in Mating Psychology

The nature of sexual reproduction over the course of human evolution guarantees that ancestral men and women encountered different reproductive opportunities and constraints: that is, in certain domains the sexes faced different adaptive *problems*, and, therefore, selection can be expected to have produced different psychological adaptations to solve those problems. In other words, one should expect male and female humans to differ in some of their psychological adaptations for the same reason that one should expect related species to differ from one another: they are adapted to solve somewhat different problems. In fact, if one considers a group of closely related species, such as the various species of macaque monkey (members of the genus *Macaca*), one could reasonably argue that the females of these species are in many ways more similar to one another than they are to the males of their own species.

Nevertheless, many social scientists continue to regard the hypothesis that human males and females differ in some of their brain mechanisms to be 'extraordinary' – like the hypothesis that certain people can bend spoons with the unaided power of their minds – and, as such, to require extraordinary evidence to be taken seriously. The reasonable, prudent, parsimonious assumption, many social scientists believe, is that human male and female brains are essentially identical. But to anyone whose view of life is informed even minimally by Darwinism, the probability that human male and female psychologies are essentially identical is so close to zero as to be indistinguishable from it. To the adaptationist, the reasonable, prudent, parsimonious assumption is that the sexes differ in certain aspects of their psychologies as profoundly as they do in certain aspects of more easily observed portions of their anatomies.

Consider, for example, the fact that ancestral males would never have been 100 per cent certain of paternity: that is, they faced the potential problem of being cuckolded and, consequently, of investing in another man's child, which would have been highly maladaptive. Ancestral females, on the other hand, never faced this problem, as their confidence in maternity was always 100 per cent. Therefore, we should expect selection to have favoured anti-cuckoldry psychological adaptations in males but not in females.

Ancestral men and women also differed dramatically in the minimum possible investments they could make in an offspring if that offspring was to have a chance of surviving to reproductive age. For an ancestral female, the minimum possible investment consisted of an egg cell, nine months of gestation, the perils of childbirth, several years of nursing, and continuing but diminishing care and provisioning after weaning until the child was old enough to survive on its own. As ancestral males invested substantially in their wives' offspring, their *typical* parental investments were very high (by mammalian standards); nevertheless, their *minimum possible* investment consisted merely of the contents of a single ejaculate and a few minutes of time. In other words, ancestral males could have reproduced at almost no cost if they impregnated a woman to whom they were not married and sired a child in whom they did not invest, and such low-cost reproduction would have been highly adaptive. Ancestral females, on the other hand, never encountered an opportunity for low-cost reproduction: the minimum possible female parental investment was very large. Selection would therefore have favoured in men, but not in women, psychological adaptations that function to promote the pursuit of low-cost reproductive opportunities.

Consider an ancestral hunter-gatherer man with one wife, whom he married when she was nubile and who bore four children during her reproductive career. If he sired just one additional child by another woman during his lifetime, he increased his reproductive success by an enormous 25 per cent (and this may have had little, if any, detrimental effect on his wife's reproductive success). However, if one of his wife's children was sired by another man, she still had only four offspring (and her husband's reproductive success was diminished by 25 per cent). This line of reasoning definitely does *not* imply that it was maladaptive for ancestral women ever to have affairs. If that were the case, ancestral men would have had no opportunities to have affairs and, hence, there would have been no adaptive advantage to desiring them. But the benefits that women derived from 'extra-pair copulations' would have been in the form of acquiring additional material resources, trading up in the husband market, or producing children of higher genetic quality, not in the form of *additional* children.

Sex with strangers

Given the ineluctable sex differences in reproductive opportunities and constraints that we have just sketched, it is reasonable to propose the following hypothesis: during the course of human evolutionary history it was *always* adaptive for a man to copulate with any fertile woman (other than his close kin) as long as the risks were low enough, whereas it was *never* adaptive for a woman to copulate with just any fertile man. (We stress again that it was sometimes adaptive for ancestral women to copulate with men other than their husbands – but not without regard to the men's characteristics, the husband's characteristics and the woman's particular circumstances.)

Random matings with anonymous strangers would have been fitness disasters for ancestral women, entailing large costs and few, if any, benefits.

By using the words 'always' and 'never' in the previous paragraph, we implied the existence of stark, qualitative differences between the selection pressures operating on ancestral men and women. If we are right, selection might well have favoured similarly stark, qualitative differences between certain male and female psychological adaptations. In particular, we might reasonably expect men and women to differ profoundly in their motivations to have sex with strangers. Do such sex differences actually exist?

Diverse kinds of evidence can be brought to bear on this and similar questions. One approach has been to ask experimental subjects (usually college students) about their sexual desires and inclinations. For example, the psychologist David Buss asked single university students how many sexual partners they would like to have within various time periods, ranging from 'next month' to 'your lifetime'. Men reported that they would like to have many more partners during every interval than women did: for example, men said that during the next year they would like to have an average of six partners, whereas women said that they would like to have an average of one partner.

Because sexual intercourse exposes men and women to dramatically different risks (such as pregnancy) or different degrees of risk (such as sexually transmitted diseases, reputation and violent retaliation by a jealous mate), sex differences of the kind that Buss found may to some extent result from a conscious appraisal of such risks rather than from sex differences in sexual desires *per se*. One way to test this hypothesis is to ask subjects to imagine how they would behave in circumstances in which these risks were absent. If men and women really do differ in their sexual desires, one would expect significant sex differences to persist even in an imagined, risk-free world.

Following this line of reasoning, in *The Evolution of Human Sexuality* Symons predicted that a sex difference would be found if married subjects were asked the following question: 'If the opportunity presented itself to have sexual intercourse with an anonymous member of the opposite sex who was as competent a lover as your partner but no more so, and who was as physically attractive as your partner but no more so, and there was *no* risk of pregnancy, discovery, or disease, and *no* chance of forming a more durable relationship, do you think you would do so?' A decade later, Symons and Bruce Ellis administered a questionnaire containing this question, among many others, to college students who had steady partners (though few were actually married). As predicted, highly significant sex differences emerged. For example, 17 per cent of male and only 4 per cent of female subjects answered 'certainly would', while 20 per cent of male and 50 per cent of female subjects answered 'certainly would not'.

While interviews and questionnaires have the advantage of directly measuring attitudes and beliefs and asking the particular questions that researchers are interested in, they also have the disadvantages of being intrusive, of creating attitudes, of eliciting atypical responses and of being limited to accessible subjects. Even though questionnaires about sexual desires and inclinations are always completed anonymously, subjects may nonetheless trim their sails to the breeze of perceived social expectations. Furthermore, no matter how dutifully subjects strive to sound themselves within and to answer the questions honestly, it is difficult or impossible to know what one would do in circumstances one has never actually encountered. These and similar arguments have been emphasized by critics who believe that questionnaire and survey responses systematically exaggerate the differences between men's and women's sexualities. When answering these kinds of questions, the argument goes, women may be reluctant to reveal their socially unacceptable libidinous desires, whereas men may exaggerate their sexual appetitites in order to present themselves as macho studs.

We agree that questionnaires and surveys have serious scientific limitations; but we disagree with the notion that such research systematically tends to exaggerate sex differences. On the contrary, we will argue that exactly the opposite is true – that is, that men and women differ much more profoundly than one would infer from their answers to questions about what they would like to do, or what they think they would do, or what they think other people would do in certain situations.

In the studies we have just described, although the

predicted sex differences were found, and these differences were highly significant in a *statistical* sense, there was also substantial overlap between the sexes. In fact, one way of interpreting these data is that they *fail* to support the hypothesis that in certain domains males and females possess qualitatively different psychological adaptations. Rather, they seem to imply that the sexes merely differ quantitatively, much as they do, for example, in height (on average, men are taller than women, but the two height distributions overlap substantially).

However, when one considers 'real world' manifestations of human sexual psychology, rather than questionnaire and survey data about sexual desires and inclinations, men and women appear to differ profoundly, and in precisely the predicted ways. We will review four kinds of real world evidence, consisting of one planned and three unplanned or 'natural' experiments. In this chapter we discuss (a) 'Would you go to bed with me tonight?', an experiment by Russell Clark and Elaine Hatfield; (b) prostitution; and (c) the sexual behaviour of lesbians and gay men. In the following chapters we will consider in greater depth a fourth line of evidence: commercial erotica.

'Would you go to bed with me tonight?'

In the course of many interviews with young, single men concerning their sexual desires and attitudes, Elaine Hatfield, a prominent American sex researcher, rarely encountered sexual braggadocio or macho posturing. On the contrary, most men expressed serious reservations and misgivings about dating 'easy' women. The men worried, for example, that the women might be easy to get but hard to get rid of; that the women might embarrass them in public; that they (the men) might be teased by their friends; that they might acquire a sexually transmitted disease; and so forth. Hatfield wondered, however, what men and women would do if they actually encountered a low-cost sexual opportunity in real life rather than in the realm of the imagination. To find out, she and Russell Clark conducted two identical – now classic – experiments on the campus of Florida State University (the first in 1978, the second in 1982, before there was significant public awareness of AIDS).

Clark and Hatfield's methodology is worth reviewing in some detail. Five college women and four college men served as the experimenters' confederates. These confederates were about twenty-two years old, were casually but neatly dressed, and varied in attractiveness from 'slightly unattractive' to 'moderately attractive' (variation in confederate attractiveness had no demonstrable effect on the experiments' results). Confederates approached opposite-sex subjects (all strangers) who were alone at one of five campus locations. There were 48 men and 48 women subjects in each experiment, a total of 96 male and 96 female subjects. All approaches occurred on weekdays (when subjects were less likely to have a date that night), during good weather and not between classes. Confederates were instructed to approach only people whom they personally found sexually attractive.

Consequently, the subjects tended to be physically attractive: the women confederates rated the average male subject as 7.3 in attractiveness on a 9-point scale, while the male confederates rated the average female subject as 7.7.

The confederate said to the subject, 'I have been noticing you around campus. I find you to be very attractive.' Then the confederate asked one of three randomly selected questions (during the course of each study, each question was asked 32 times):

- Would you go out with me tonight?
  (The Date condition)
- Would you come over to my apartment tonight?
  (The Apartment condition)
- Would you go to bed with me tonight?
  (The Bed condition)

We invite the reader, before proceeding further, to predict what percentage of men and women subjects complied with each of these requests. We make this suggestion because the results of this and similar studies often seem obvious – or even trivial – in retrospect. But they are not obvious or trivial at all. We have found, in our own classrooms, that if we give our students the methodological details of Clark and Hatfield's experiment and then ask them to predict the results (on a form we provide), few predictions are even in the ballpark and virtually none is really on the money. The actual results were as follows.

Percentage of subjects complying with each request

Subjects	Date	Apartment	Bed
Female	53	3	0
Male	50	69	72

When American university students were asked for a date by a presentable opposite-sex stranger, about half of each sex accepted. But when subjects were asked for sex (which presumably was implicit in the 'Apartment' condition), men were significantly *more* likely to accept, whereas women's acceptance rate plummeted nearly to zero (the 'Bed' condition actually was zero). Men and women subjects also differed diametrically in their reactions to being asked for sex by a stranger. Typical men's comments included 'Why do we have to wait until tonight?' and 'I can't tonight, but tomorrow would be fine.' The minority of men who declined the request usually apologized, saying, for example, 'I'm married' or 'I'm going with someone.' No woman apologized for declining the request; on the contrary, their typical comments included 'You've got to be kidding' and 'What's wrong with you? Leave me alone!' In sum, when men and women encountered an actual opportunity to have sex with a stranger – rather than simply imagining such an opportunity – most men and no women complied, despite the bizarreness of the request and the risk that compliance might plausibly be thought to entail (such as being set up for a robbery).

Prostitution

Not only will most men have sex with an anonymous stranger when they have the opportunity to do so, but many are willing to pay for it – hence 'the world's oldest profession'. There are millions of prostitutes worldwide, male as well as female, and in all times and places the overwhelming majority of them service men. (Male prostitutes who service women do exist, of course, but their numbers are comparatively minuscule.) The phenomenon of prostitution is sometimes said to be rooted in men's feelings about or attitudes towards women (such as disrespect, hostility or contempt). If this were true, one would expect male homosexual prostitution not to exist – but it does; or, at least, one would expect homosexual and heterosexual prostitution to differ significantly – but they do not. Prostitution, in short, is not a window into men's feelings about or attitudes towards women; it is a window into the nature of male sexuality.

When a man purchases a prostitute's services, he is not just paying for sex; usually he is paying for *just* sex. That is, he is paying for sex without commitment, obligation, wooing, courtship, chatting up or even the 'payment' of attention. A few years ago in Los Angeles a high-end prostitution ring was publicly exposed, along with a list of some of its rich and powerful clients, and the question was raised: why would a rich, handsome, famous man pay a woman $1500 for sex when he could walk into any bar in Beverly Hills and go home with a very attractive young woman? The answer is that he was not paying the prostitute $1500 for sex *per se*; he was paying her $1500 to go away afterwards.

We believe that the sex differences we are attempting to characterize here are actually common knowledge; but their existence is not always recognized consciously, perhaps for the same reason that fish are notorious for their inability to discover water. These differences between men's and women's sexualities are so pervasive and so much a part of the unexamined, unremarked background of everyday life that we are normally no more conscious of them than we are of the air we breathe.

Consider the following thought experiment. Ann and Andy are an imaginary, attractive couple in their early twenties. Their sex life is monogamous, active, varied, mutually satisfying and egalitarian, in the sense that they typically want to have sex equally often, are equally likely to initiate sex, are equally orgasmic during sex and are equally happy with their sexual relationship. They are, in short, exactly the sort of couple that is regularly trotted out to dispel the 'myth' that the sexes differ profoundly in their sexual psychologies. And, indeed, if we focused solely on Ann and Andy's sexual interactions with each other we might be tempted to infer that innate male–female differences in sexuality are relatively few and trivial, if they exist at all. But now imagine that one morning Ann and Andy awaken and for some mysterious reason decide that each will have sex with as many physically attractive opposite-sex strangers as they can during the next twelve hours (without paying for it).

Andy will be lucky if he is able to bed a single woman. Ann, on the other hand, will be able to bed as many men as she can physically tolerate, and, if she wishes, get paid to boot. Thus, when we broaden our perspective from Ann and Andy as an isolated couple to Ann and Andy at large in the sexual marketplace, the gulf between male and female sexual psychologies springs sharply into focus.

Homosexuals

There are many reasons why a person of either sex might choose not to have sex with strangers: for example, religious or moral objections; fear of jeopardizing an established relationship; not being sufficiently attractive to compete in the sexual marketplace; fear of sexually transmitted diseases; a preference for expending one's time and energy in other ways; or anxiety about potential financial or social repercussions (such as job loss). Nevertheless, if most men and few women enjoy the prospect and experience of sex with strangers, then we should expect to find dramatic differences between the sexual behaviours of gay men and lesbians, because homosexuals do not have to compromise with the desires and dispositions of the opposite sex in their sexual relations. In other words, if the primary reason that large numbers of heterosexual men do not regularly have sex with strangers is that few women are interested in this kind of sex, then it is reasonable to predict that many gay men will have sex with strangers, simply because they can, whereas lesbians will not.

Precise predictions about lesbian versus straight wo-men's sexual behaviour are difficult to make, although we would certainly not expect either to have frequent sex with strangers. On the one hand, one might expect lesbians to have somewhat more sexual partners, on average, than straight women do because lesbians do not risk pregnancy, are much less likely to acquire sexually transmitted diseases, are less at risk of physical coercion and, perhaps, are more open to unconventional sexual behaviours in general. Furthermore, although lesbians are obviously fundamentally women, they nonetheless, on average, may be somewhat masculinized (just as gay men, on average, may be somewhat feminized). On the other hand, one might suspect that straight women sometimes have sex earlier in a relationship than they would ideally prefer, owing to male sexual pressure or the fear that a man will lose interest if he has to wait too long for sex. If so, that might tend to increase the number of sexual partners that straight women have. So our essential prediction is this: on average, gay men will have many more sexual partners and much more sex with strangers than straight men do or than women do, whether straight or gay. Lesbians may have somewhat more or somewhat fewer partners than straight women, but women, whatever their sexual orientation, simply will not behave like gay men.

In *The Evolution of Human Sexuality*, Symons reviewed the evidence that was available in 1978 on this and related aspects of the sex lives of gay men and lesbians. Some of his conclusions were as follows:

The search for new sexual partners is a striking feature of the male homosexual world: the most frequent form of sexual activity is the one-night stand in which sex occurs, without obligation or commitment, between strangers . . . While more enduring relationships may develop from such encounters, relationships nonetheless begin with sex. (p. 293)

Like homosexual men, lesbians tend to place a great deal of importance on sex and sex-related activities . . . But lesbians form lasting, intimate, paired relationships far more frequently and easily than male homosexuals do; stable relationships are overwhelmingly preferred to any other, and monogamy is the ideal . . . Among lesbians sex is generally associated with enduring emotion and a loving partner . . . As among heterosexuals, lesbian dating and courting may lead to sexual relations; that is, a social relationship is the basis for a sexual relationship, whereas the opposite is true among male homosexuals . . . Lesbians rarely pick up partners for one-night stands, do not cruise, do not have anonymous sex in public places, and there are no lesbian baths . . . The similarity of heterosexual and lesbian relationships and their fundamental difference from the relations of male homosexuals . . . imply that the sexual proclivities of heterosexual males very rarely are manifested in behaviour. (pp. 298–9)

. . . there is enormous cross-cultural variation in sexual customs and laws and in the extent of male control [over women], yet nowhere in the world do heterosexual relations begin to approximate those typical of homosexual men. Even where women are relatively free of male constraints and children not an issue, as among lesbians, women very rarely behave sexually as men do. This suggests that, in addition to custom and law, heterosexual relations are structured to a substantial degree by the nature and interests of the human female. (p. 300)

After *The Evolution of Human Sexuality* was completed, the results of Alan Bell and Martin Weinberg's massive research project on homosexual men and women in the San Francisco Bay area was published. Nearly every male subject in this study had cruised (gone out specifically to look for a sexual partner) in the previous year, and most of their sexual partners were strangers. Less than 20 per cent of the lesbians had cruised even once. More than a quarter of the males had had more than fifty partners in the previous year, and another quarter had had between twenty and fifty. Only about a fifth had had fewer than six partners.

The majority of lesbian subjects had had either one or two partners in the previous year, and most had had fewer than ten partners during their lifetimes. Seventy-five per cent of the men had had over 100 lifetime partners, and 27 per cent had had over 1000. Very few lesbians had had 100 partners, and none had had anything approaching 1000. This study did not include heterosexuals, but the sexual histories of the lesbian subjects (such as number of partners and duration of sexual relationships) were roughly similar to the published research on the sexual behaviour of American heterosexual women.

During the 1980s and 1990s, the scourge of AIDS

drastically affected the lives of many gay men (in part by raising the cost of having sex with strangers). However, the rise of the 'Circuit' indicates that sex with strangers remains so attractive to many men that they are willing to take large risks to have it. The Circuit is a series of weekend-long dance parties for gay men held year-round across North America and Europe, at which sex with strangers is the main, though not the only, attraction. There are more than fifty Circuit parties each year, drawing tens of thousands of men. The Easter weekend 'White Party' in Palm Springs, California alone draws 20,000 men. The Circuit began in 1983 as a fundraiser for AIDS patients, and in the past few years the number and size of the constituent parties has exploded. According to the website of *Circuit Noize*, a magazine that reviews and publicizes the parties, 'a circuit party gives us the chance to escape the pressures of our day-to-day existence and to enter the altered world where man-to-man sex is not only accepted, but is celebrated'.

CHAPTER 6

•••

Commercial Eroticas: Unobtrusive Measures of Male and Female Sexual Psychologies

Many types of data can illuminate male and female sexual psychologies, and different research methods have different strengths and weaknesses. One way of compensating for some of the weaknesses of questionnaire data, discussed in the previous chapter, is to supplement them with 'unobtrusive measures' – research methods that do not require the co-operation of respondents and do not themselves contribute to the response.

A few evolution-minded researchers have employed unobtrusive measures to excellent effect. For example, the psychologists Martin Daly and Margo Wilson, in their book *The Truth About Cinderella*, used police statistics on child abuse and homicide to illuminate the psychology of parental love. The anthropologist Monique Borgerhoff Mulder used variation in brideprice to elucidate the determinants of female mate value in a traditional African society. And the biologist Gordon Orians used variation in Seattle real estate prices to shed light on human landscape preferences. The last two examples illustrate that free markets are potential gold mines of unobtrusive measures of human psychological adaptations – measures that thus far remain largely untapped.

A prime example is commercial erotica. Male-oriented pornography and female-oriented romance novels – the primary constituents of commercial erotica – are multi-billion-dollar global industries whose characteristic features have been shaped in free markets by the cumulative choices made by tens or hundreds of millions of men and women who have 'voted' with their money.

Commercial pornography probably exists in every industrialized society and in many developing societies as well. In the USA, the industry's annual revenues from video sales and rentals exceeded $4 billion in 1997, and porn videos accounted for more than 25 per cent of the total video market. The growth of the porn industry has been marked by successes that have acquired mythical proportions; for example, the film *Deep Throat* cost only $25,000 to make and rapidly became a classic, grossing more than $50 million.

Romance novels account for 40 per cent of mass market paperback sales in the USA, generating annual revenues of $4–6 billion. In 1997 almost 3000 romances were published in North America, where more than 45 million women are romance readers. Harlequin Enterprises, one of the largest publishers of romances, boasts annual worldwide sales of over 190 million books, attesting to the enormous appeal of these narratives to women everywhere.

A strength of conducting research on commercial erotica is that the design features of porn and of romances constitute unobtrusive measures of male and female sexual psychologies respectively. Real-life heterosexual interactions must inevitably compromise and hence blur differences between male and female sexual desires and dispositions, but erotica has no need for such compromises, since it is targeted to sex-specific audiences.

A limitation of such research, however, is that the characteristics of commercial erotica (especially porn) are determined by factors in addition to consumer preferences, including the skill and imagination of the producers, legal constraints, available technologies and production costs. For example, many aspects of commercially successful porn videos with low production values clearly do not represent the unconstrained ideal from the standpoint of maximizing male sexual arousal, but rather the cost-effective ideal from the standpoint of maximizing pornographers' profits. As a result, commercial erotica may fail to identify certain features of male and female sexual psychologies that are of theoretical interest. Experimental and questionnaire research methods, by contrast, allow for a broader range of hypothesis testing and can be used to probe dimensions of male and female sexual psychologies that are not manifested in commercial erotica. Fortunately, obtrusive and unobtrusive measures can complement each other, to the extent that the weaknesses of one tend to be the strengths of the other.

One way in which erotica can be used to illuminate human sexual psychologies is to compare commercially successful products with less successful ones. Indeed, in a recent collection of essays on the nature of the romance novel by the women who write them, *Dangerous Men and Adventurous Women*, many of the authors noted that sales figures and royalty cheques provide reliable information about women's psychology. Best-selling romance novels, for example, almost never feature gentle, sensitive heroes, because women readers prefer to fantasize about strong, confident men who ultimately are tamed only by their love for the heroine. *Gone with the Wind* is a classic example of the popularity of a strong hero; in the end, it is Rhett Butler whom Scarlett desires, not the wimpy Ashley. Romance writers who have experimented with gentle, sensitive heroes have not been rewarded in the marketplace.

Another approach is to attempt to identify the essential ingredients of erotic genres, to distil their essences. For example, a common characteristic of pornographic videos is (attempted) humour, but humour is *not* an essential ingredient. Many thousands of humourless porn videos are commercially successful. In contrast, as discussed below, impersonal sex *is* an essential ingredient of porn videos.

A third approach, which we will expand on in the following chapters in our discussion of slash fiction, is to analyse smaller, more esoteric erotic genres and to compare them to the mainstream forms. The logic behind this approach is that apparent exceptions can prove (that is, test) the rules, can highlight the essential ingredients in male and female eroticas, and can inspire testable hypotheses about the causes of within-sex variation in erotic preferences.

Pornography

The utopian male fantasy realm depicted in pornography – which historian Steven Marcus dubbed 'pornotopia' – remains essentially unchanged through time and space. In pornotopia, sex is sheer lust and physical gratification, devoid of courtship, commitment, durable relationships or mating effort. It is a world in which women are eager to have sex with strangers, easily sexually aroused and always orgasmic (that is, the depiction of women's sexual pleasure, real or feigned, is an essential ingredient of mainstream porn). Porn videos contain minimal plot development, focusing instead on the sex acts themselves and emphasizing the display of female bodies, especially close-ups of faces (displaying sexual arousal), breasts and genitals. The fact that videos and, in the last few years, the internet so thoroughly dominate male-oriented erotica testifies to the deeply visual nature of male sexuality. Men tend to be sexually aroused by 'objectified' visual stimuli. As a consequence, porn videos do not require the existence of a point-of-view character to be effective, and scenes of a woman alone, masturbating, are relatively common. The male viewer imagines taking the sexually aroused woman out of the scene and having sex with her. Women porn stars manifest cues of high mate value in that they are young and physically attractive. Pornotopia, in short, is a world of low-cost, impersonal sex with an endless succession of lustful, beautiful, orgasmic women.

Like prostitution, porn is often said to evidence male contempt for, or lack of respect for, women. And, as discussed above with respect to prostitution, there exists an ideal test case for such claims: gay male porn. If these claims were accurate, we would expect gay male porn either not to exist at all or, if it did exist, to differ in significant ways from straight male porn (it might, for example, emphasize the development of enduring relationships or be less relentlessly focused on genitals). But, in fact, gay and straight porn are essentially identical, differing only in the sex of the actors. In fact, gay porn often gives the impression of being more 'real' than straight porn does: for one thing, the actors in gay porn almost invariably seem to be having a genuinely good time, which is not always true of the actresses in straight porn; for another, the impersonal sex depicted in gay porn is not very different from the real-life sexual relations of many gay men.

The romance novel

Although the romance novel has been called, with some justification, 'women's pornography', if male-oriented video porn could be said to have an opposite, the romance novel would be it. The goal of a romance novel's heroine is never sex for its own sake, much less impersonal sex with strangers. The core of a romance novel's plot is a love story in the course of which the heroine overcomes obstacles to identify, win the heart of, and ultimately marry the one man who is right for her. That is why there cannot be romance serials featuring the same heroine, as there can be endless iterations of James Bond adventures; each romance must end with the establishment of a permanent union. Unlike male-oriented porn, the existence of a point-of-view character with whom the reader subjectively identifies is an essential feature of romance fiction. The heroine is always the main point-of-view character, but in many successful romances the point of view shifts back and forth between heroine and hero (implying that readers of mainstream romances do not have a problem identifying with the subjective experiences of an ostensibly male character). The romance novel is at once women's erotica and women's adventure fiction.

Romances vary dramatically in the extent to which sexual activity is depicted, from not-at-all to highly explicit descriptions. In other words, although the description of sexual activities is common in romances, it is *not* an essential ingredient. When sex *is* described, it serves the plot rather than dominating it. The hero discovers in the heroine a fulfilling focus for his passion, which binds him to her and ensures his future fidelity. Sex scenes depict the heroine's control of the hero, not her sexual submissiveness. Sexual activity is described subjectively, primarily through the heroine's emotions, rather than through her physical responses or through visual imagery, and the heroine is sexually aroused tactually rather than visually. The emotional focus of a romance is on love, commitment, domesticity and nurturing. In her ethnography of a group of American romance novel readers, Janice Radway reported that her subjects were angry about men's tastes for impersonal sex and sexual variety, and these women did not want to adopt male standards, in real life or in their erotica; they wanted men to adopt their standards.

We are not aware of evidence on the question of whether women readers use romances to enhance masturbation, as men use porn (Radway asked her subjects about this, but they wouldn't answer); but readers clearly derive sexual satisfaction from reading romances. Coles and Shamp compared readers and non-readers of romances on various personality and demographic measures and found no differences between the two groups except that readers engaged in sexual intercourse much more frequently than non-readers did, and readers were much more likely than non-readers to use fantasies to enhance intercourse.

The characteristics of the heroes of successful romances shed considerable light on the psychology of female mate choice. As mentioned earlier, these romances almost never feature gentle, sensitive heroes. One highly successful romance writer noted that women prefer to fantasize about 'a strong, dominant, aggressive male brought to the point of surrender by a woman'.

The anthropologist April Gorry analysed every description of the heroes of forty-five romance novels. Each of the novels in her sample had been independently nominated for its excellence by at least three romance readers or writers. The results of Gorry's research serve as an important corrective to the widespread belief – even among evolutionary psychologists – that women evaluate potential mates primarily on the bases of money and socioeconomic status.

In all, or almost all, of the romances that Gorry analysed, the hero was older than the heroine, by an average of seven years in the twenty novels in which their ages were given exactly. Heroes were always described as taller than the heroine, and in forty-four of the forty-five novels heroes were described as 'tall', often as being over 6 feet, or as 6' 2", or, in one case, as 6' 3". In other words, romance heroes are much taller than the heroine and taller than the average man, but not too tall. The adjectives used most frequently to describe the physical characteristics of heroes were: muscular (45 novels), handsome (44), strong (42), large (35), tanned (35), masculine (33) and energetic (32). That a particular adjective was not mentioned explicitly in a particular novel, however, does *not* imply that the hero possessed the opposite trait. In not a single case was a hero described as short, skinny, fat, non-muscular, ugly, weak, small, pale, effeminate or lethargic.

Gorry also found that romance heroes exhibited cues of physical and social 'competence'. Heroes were described as sexually bold (40 novels), calm (39), confident (39) and impulsive (34); no hero was described as sexually inhibited, nervous, timid, clumsy, or fearful in the face of a life-threatening challenge. In thirty-eight novels the hero was described as 'intelligent', and no heroes were described as unintelligent, although six lacked formal education.

The characteristics of heroes that were described most consistently had to do with their feelings for the heroines: sexually desirous (45); declares his love (45); wants the heroine more than he has ever wanted a woman (45); has never been so deeply in love (45); experiences intrusive thoughts about the heroine (44); is gentle with the heroine (but not in general) (44); considers the heroine unique (43); wants to protect the heroine (41); is possessive of the heroine (39); is sexually jealous of the heroine (36) (and, of course, no hero is described as having the opposite of any of these traits). These feelings are virtually a textbook list of the characteristics that, as the anthropologist Helen Yonie Harris has documented, universally constitute the experience of romantic love.

The essential characteristics of the hero of a successful romance novel thus have to do primarily with his physical appearance, physical and social competence and intense love for the heroine. In contrast, being rich and having high socioeconomic standing, while surely more common among romance heroes than among the general run of men, are *not* essential characteristics. In Gorry's research, heroes had a high social rank or occupation in twenty-three novels, but had a low social rank or occupation in five novels; and although the hero was rich in nineteen novels, he was poor in ten. When considering the psychological adaptations that underpin human female mate choice, it is worth bearing in mind that money, social classes and formal education did not exist for the overwhelming majority of human evolutionary history. The heroes of successful romance novels may or may not be rich, aristocratic or well educated, but they consistently possess characteristics that would have made them highly desirable mates during the course of human evolutionary history; they are tall, strong, handsome, healthy, intelligent, confident, competent, 'dangerous' men whose love for the heroine ensures that she and her children will reap the benefits of these sterling qualities.

Several contributors to *Dangerous Men and Adventurous Women* argue explicitly or implicitly that the characteristics shared by the heroes of successful romances illuminate evolved female mating psychology. Robyn Donald's essay is the most explicit in this respect. She writes:

Until very recently in our historic past, strong, successful, powerful men had the greatest prospects of fathering children who survived. If a woman formed a close bond with a man who was sensible, competent and quick-witted, one high up in the family or tribal pecking order, a man with the ability to provide for her and any children she might have, the chances of her children surviving were greater than those of a woman whose mate was inefficient.

Romance heroes are 'warriors', not necessarily in the literal sense of the word, but in the sense that they possess the physical, intellectual and temperamental qualities of successful warriors.

In sum, the realm of the romance novel, which one might call 'romantopia', is a utopian, erotic female counter-fantasy to pornotopia. Just as porn actresses exhibit a suspiciously male-like sexuality, romances are, in Janice Radway's words, 'exercises in the imaginative transformation of masculinity to conform with female standards'. Like Clark and Hatfield's experiments, prostitution and the sex lives of gay men and lesbians, the essential ingredients of porn and romance novels imply the existence of deep and abiding differences between male and female mating psychologies.

The psychological significance of commercial eroticas

We argued above that throughout the course of human evolutionary history most successful reproduction occurred within marriages, and most marriages were monogamous economic and child-rearing partnerships based on a division of labour. But if this account is correct, at least in its general outline, how is it possible for male and female sexual psychologies to differ as dramatically as commercial eroticas would seem to imply they do?

The answer, as sketched earlier, is that ancestral men and women differed qualitatively in some of the adaptive problems that they encountered in the domain of mating. However similar men's and women's *typical* parental investments may have been, the sexes differed starkly in their minimum possible investments. If a man sired a child in whom he did not invest, he could have reproduced at almost no cost. Even if such opportunities did not come along often in ancestral human populations, capitalizing on them when they did come along was so adaptive that males evolved a sexual psychology that makes low-cost sex with new women exciting both to imagine and to engage in, and that motivates men to create such sexual opportunities. Pornotopia is a fantasy realm, made possible by evolutionarily novel technologies, in which impersonal sex with a succession of high-mate-value women is the norm rather than the rare exception.

Ancestral females, by contrast, had nothing to gain and much to lose from engaging in impersonal sex with random strangers and from seeking sexual variety for its own sake, and they had a great deal to gain from choosing their mates carefully. The romance novel is a chronicle of female mate choice in which the heroine overcomes obstacles to identify, win and marry the hero, who embodies the physical, psychological and social characteristics that constituted high male mate value during the course of human evolutionary history.

But why, one might wonder, is there no commercial erotic genre that combines the ingredients of pornotopia and romantopia, thereby doubling the potential audience and the potential profit? After all, women are sexual as well as romantic beings, fully capable of being physically aroused by hard-core sex scenes. (In fact, a significant proportion of porn video rentals are to women, almost all of whom use them to enhance sexual activities with their partners, not to enhance solitary masturbation.) Also, the evidence of romance novels would seem to imply that women, like men, prefer erotica in which the sexual partners are new to each other rather than being an established couple. And men, for their part, are romantic as well as sexual beings who fall in love as regularly as women do. Choosing mates carefully and establishing long-term mateships were adaptive problems faced by *both* sexes, not just females, throughout human evolutionary history.

Many commercially successful romantic comedies and romantic adventures do, in fact, appeal to both sexes, and men and women alike can enjoy the literary works of a Jane Austen; but the unisex appeal of such films and novels is gained at the cost of failing to embody many of pornotopia's and romantopia's essential ingredients. One could imagine, however, a film genre that combined a number of the ingredients of romantopia, pornotopia and mainstream commercial cinema, such as romantic comedies and romantic adventures with compelling plots, intelligent and witty dialogue, fully developed characters, first-rate acting, physically attractive stars, happily-ever-after endings and hard-core sex scenes. Such films, however, would not be commercially viable; they would be very expensive to produce, could not be widely distributed and would jeopardize the careers of those who participated in them.

But even if such films were produced, we do not believe that they would eliminate the markets for porn and romances, because some of the essential ingredients of pornotopia and romantopia are mutually incompatible. Most obviously, impersonal sex, pornotopia's core fantasy, is anathema to romantopia. The 'plot' of a porn film or video is rarely more than a feebly connected sequence of sex scenes, each of which typically ends with an external ejaculation, the 'money shot'. A porn video has almost as many climaxes as it does scenes, but a romance novel has only one climax, the moment when the hero and the heroine declare their mutual love for one another.

CHAPTER 7

....

Slash Fiction

As noted in the Prologue, 'slash fiction' refers to romantic/erotic narratives, written almost exclusively by and for women, in which both protagonists are expropriated male media characters, the co-stars of various police, detective, adventure, spy and science-fiction television series or literary works (such as Sherlock Holmes and Dr Watson). Popular pairings include Kirk and Spock from the original *Star Trek* series, Starsky and Hutch from the show of the same name, Bodie and Doyle from *The Professionals*, Illya and Napoleon from *The Man from UNCLE* and Jim and Blair from *The Sentinel*. Although slash protagonists fall in love with and have sex with each other, they are usually depicted as heterosexual (however improbable this may seem to those unfamiliar with the

genre), sometimes as bisexual and occasionally as homosexual. The term 'slash' arose from the convention of
using a stroke or slash between the men's names to
signify their relationship (such as Kirk/Spock, or K/S).

The history of slash

Slash as a body of literature disseminated among members of a community grew out of *Star Trek* fandom in the
mid-1970s. Female fans began to write stories set in the
fictional realm of *Star Trek* in which the bond between
Kirk and Spock is deeper than any other. In the course of
these tales, Kirk and Spock become lovers, overcoming
many obstacles that are placed in their path.

Despite opposition from some *Star Trek* fans, who
disapproved of this version of their heroes, K/S zines
(short for 'fanzines', which itself is short for 'fan
magazines' – collections of fan-produced stories) continue to be produced to this day, some very profession-
ally, with slick cover artwork and spiral or perfect
binding. They were, and for the most part still are, sold
by mail order and at fan conventions.

Slash is by no means a peculiarly American phenomenon; nor was it created by a single person. It seems to
have arisen spontaneously at about the same time in
various places in the USA, Canada, Germany, Australia
and the UK. The most popular pairings immediately to
follow K/S came from the American cop show *Starsky
and Hutch* and the British television shows *Blake's Seven*
and *The Professionals* (and some of the most popular

writers of Bodie/Doyle slash were British and Australian). Slash fans write, edit and publish hundreds of stories, and also produce artwork and novels, in a cottage industry that has benefited enormously from the advent of desktop publishing and cheap photocopying.

Through the 1970s and 1980s, when slash consisted mainly of print zines (advertised in adzines as well as at conventions), the community of slash readers and writers in the USA was relatively small, with a core of perhaps 500 active fans. Print runs for most zines were in the order of 200 to 600, with some selling up to a thousand copies. The slash community has recently seen the reprinting of some of these older zines, which are now considered classics.

In her book *Enterprising Women*, the ethnographer Camille Bacon-Smith used her interviews with a sample of women who attended a New England slash convention to characterize the community of slash fans of the 1980s. She concluded that virtually all were female, and that most had university degrees and were middle class, single, white and heterosexual (lesbian and bisexual slash fans exist in about the same proportions as in the general population). Although her subjects ranged in age from twenty to seventy, most were in their thirties. Today this may be changing as a result of the influx of new, young fans who are discovering slash on the internet. Enter the word 'slash' into any search engine and you will find hundreds of websites containing slash stories for many male/male pairings (most sites being dedicated to just one or two TV shows and pairs). Some sites also advertise conventions and zine publishers. It is thus difficult to estimate how many people currently read slash. All one can be sure of is that the number is steadily increasing as more girls and women become aware of the existence of slash and gain cheap, easy access to it.

In Japan there is a similar genre of male/male romances, written largely by and for females, with sales in the millions: the girls' comic books *shounen ai* (boys' love), which are also referred to as *yaoi*, particularly with respect to the amateur works. The young female audience of *shounen ai* is also largely responsible for the popularity of this type of story in amateur *manga* (comic or graphic novels). *Shounen ai* stories describe the development of love relationships between boys or very young men that closely parallel (except for the youth of the protagonists) those between fully adult men in Western slash. They also resemble mainstream romances in that one boy is the pursuer and the other the pursued, until the latter relents and accepts their mutual love. One *manga* that is not a *shounen ai*, *Eroika yori ai wo komete* ('From Eroica with Love') by Yasuko Aoike, has actually become incorporated into Western slash, the resulting stories branching off from the Japanese original. These stories chronicle the adventures of an English thief, Dorian, and the German NATO officer, Klaus, whom he loves and pursues. Another popular *yaoi*, *Zetsuai*, and its sequel, *Bronze*, by Minami Ozaki, chronicle the relationship between a rock star and the soccer star with whom he falls obsessively in love. In its popularity, it is reminiscent of Anne Rice's well-known novels about the vampire Lestat, which also touch on the theme of love between men, though more obliquely than *Zetsuai* does.

Academic views: romance and pornography, rewritten, retooled

Most academic interest in slash stories and the women who write and read them has come from the areas of media studies and cultural studies, the former tending to emphasize the pornographic aspects of slash, the latter its romantic aspects. In one of the earliest academic articles on slash, 'Pornography by Women, for Women, with Love', Joanna Russ documented the existence of male/male romance stories in the form of K/S. She focused on the life-long monogamous relationships depicted in most K/S and argued that slash represents a new kind of pornography, written by and for women, wherein sex is a vehicle for the portrayal of character. She noted that slash stories are about lovers who take a 'personal interest in each other's minds, not only each other's bodies' and who develop an 'exclusive commitment to one another'. While many slash stories contain detailed descriptions of sexual acts, the emphasis is on the emotional qualities of these acts, in stark contrast to the impersonal couplings of male-oriented pornography. Russ also perceptively observed that these stories are not really about male homosexuality; rather, they depict a female version of sexuality acted out on and by male bodies.

Early K/S stories (which were Russ's focus) describe

easy anal intercourse without the use of lubricants as well as simultaneous and multiple orgasms, perhaps implying that the writers of these stories were not actually imagining male/male anal intercourse. When slash writers learned that their sex scenes contained these sorts of technical errors, they did their homework (for example, studying Alex Comfort's *The Joy of Gay Sex*) and their descriptions of sexual activities became more realistic. For example, a writer might place a tube of hand lotion or lubricant in a bedside cabinet, making it conveniently available when the protagonists need it. However, the increased technical sophistication with which slash writers portray male/male sex does not necessarily imply that their underlying fantasy has itself been changed.

In 'Romantic Myth, Transcendence, and *Star Trek* Zines', Patricia Fraser Lamb and Dianna Veith argued that slash is really a type of androgynous romance, a reworking of romance conventions to create a loving relationship between equals, which, they believe, cannot exist between men and women in a patriarchal society. They emphasize the telepathic bond that Kirk and Spock often share in K/S stories, and they note that these characters mix and match traditional masculine and feminine traits.

The two most widely read academic writers on slash, other than Bacon-Smith, are Constance Penley and Henry Jenkins. Penley has proposed several explanations of why women write such narratives, including the hypotheses that slash readers and writers are 'alienated' from their own bodies, that the slash pairing avoids the inherent inequalities of the romance-novel formula, and that slash fans are 'retooling' masculinity by creating sensitive but not wimpy protagonists. She also emphasizes 'multiple identification', as evidenced by the shifting point of view that is commonplace in slash fiction. In Penley's view, the fact that slash pairs are usually portrayed as heterosexual (in that theirs is the only same-sex sexual relationship that either has experienced) coupled with the possibility of multiple identification allows the heterosexual female reader to identify with a male character and still 'have' him sexually, since by being heterosexual a slash protagonist is, in a sense, 'not unavailable' to women.

Jenkins' book *Textual Poachers: Television Fans and Participatory Culture* covers more than just slash stories. It discusses fan-produced stories, artwork, films and music videos – slash and otherwise. It is also the academic work most favoured by slash fans themselves. Jenkins focuses on the ways in which fans interpret and 'rewrite' mass media. In his chapter 'Welcome to Bisexuality, Captain Kirk' he reviews the major arguments of academic students of slash (such as slash as pornography for women, slash as androgynous romance and slash as allowing multiple identifications in fantasy) and then presents his own views on the connection between the great male/male friendship theme of much eighteenth- and nineteenth-century fiction (friendships so strong that the friends would give their lives for each other) and the narrative structure of slash. He describes the typical slash story as moving from an initial relationship (normally friendship) to a crisis of communication (triggered when one of the men realizes that he loves his friend) to a confession of love to a reconfirmation and deepening of the relationship through sex. Like most students of slash, he notes that its central themes are intimacy and commitment, and he argues that 'slash is not so much a genre about sex as it is a genre about the limitations of traditional masculinity and about reconfiguring male identity'.

Our research on romance readers

When people first learn of the existence of slash fiction, many are baffled and bewildered (as was this book's second author: see the Prologue). Why, they wonder, would any woman want to read love stories – whether or not they feature media characters and contain graphic sex scenes – in which both protagonists are men? Implicit in this question may be the assumption that most women would not easily identify with a male character, despite the fact that movie-goers of both sexes and all ages seem to identify easily with men, women, children, talking pigs, cartoon characters and animated desk lamps. But perhaps it is not the fact that slash fans identify with male characters that seems so perplexing; rather, it is the fact that they do so specifically in the context of a romantic/sexual relationship.

One might hypothesize that slash fans differ from most women in that the former have some sort of psycho-sexual quirk, which the latter lack, that facilitates identification with male characters in a romantic/sexual relationship. To test this hypothesis, we asked the members of a mainstream romance readers' group, none of whom had previously read a male/male romance (slash or otherwise) to read a male/male romance novel and then to complete a lengthy questionnaire designed to elicit their reactions to the novel, their views on romances, and various kinds of personal and demographic information.

Our 'test' novel was *The Catch Trap* by Marion Zimmer Bradley, a male/male romance in which the protagonists are original creations rather than a media pairing. A slash novel would have been completely inappropriate for our purposes, because slash is, first and foremost, fan fiction. The slash writer can and does assume that her readers are intimately familiar with the fictional setting and characters in her story, hence she does not need to supply these dramatic elements. To really appreciate a work of slash fiction one must be familiar with the show from which it is derived, one must like the show and one must find at least one of the male leads attractive. It is extremely unlikely that any example of slash would have met these criteria for a majority of our subjects.

As the author of *The Catch Trap* was a well-known science-fiction/fantasy writer, and the book had sold reasonably well (it was in its seventh printing), we decided that it would be an ideal test novel. Its protagonists are two trapeze artists (a flyer and a catcher) who work together and eventually fall in love: Mario is older, darker in colouring, larger, less in touch with his emotions and more sexually experienced than his partner, Tommy. Although Mario and Tommy's relationship eventually becomes sexual, *The Catch Trap* (like many romances and some slash) does not contain graphic descriptions of sexual activities.

One of the questions we asked our subjects was: 'Compared to other romances you have read, how much did you enjoy *The Catch Trap*?' Seventy-eight per cent reported enjoying the test novel at least as much as they enjoy most mainstream romances, and significantly more subjects said that they enjoyed the novel 'somewhat more than average' than said they enjoyed it 'somewhat less than average'. Although this was but one small study, we believe that this finding is so clear-cut that for all intents and purposes it refutes the 'psychosexual quirk' explanation of slash. That is, most women who read romances, not just slash fans, can enjoy a male/male romance and identify with one or both protagonists.

We also looked to see what subject characteristics correlated with degree of enjoying/not enjoying the test novel. Characteristics that did *not* correlate with degree of enjoyment included marital status, importance of religion and importance of having children. Some of the characteristics that *did* correlate with degree of enjoyment will not be very surprising; for example, subjects who liked the novel tended to be younger, were not homophobic, found both Mario and Tommy appealing and believed that the protagonists' love was strong and would last.

Other correlations, however, are less obvious and more interesting. Subjects who said they enjoyed *The Catch Trap* more than the average romance were more likely to report that they had been considered tomboys when they were girls. (And this was *not* merely a by-product of their youth, as there was no correlation between subject age and having been considered a tomboy.) Subjects who enjoyed the novel were also more likely to report that they enjoy buddy, action, science-fiction and horror movies, and they were especially attracted to Mario and Tommy's working partnership.

In addition, almost every subject who enjoyed *The Catch Trap* said that she would have enjoyed it as much if the sex scenes (which were very tame by mainstream romance and slash standards) had been more graphic, suggesting that these women, like slash fans, enjoy explicit descriptions of sexual activities when they occur in the context of a loving relationship. In the next chapter, we will discuss our views on the significance of these findings.

CHAPTER 8

••

Women's Mating Psychology: Lessons from Slash

In Chapter 2 we described the central role that *comparison* plays in the adaptationist programme. Comparison is crucial in using women's erotica to illuminate evolved female mating psychology because the features shared by *all* forms of women's erotica are much more likely to reflect psychological adaptations than are the variable features.

Academic students of slash, while always interesting and often insightful, have sometimes reached erroneous conclusions because they did not cast their nets widely enough, even within the genre of slash itself. For example, some theorists have written about slash as if it consisted only of Kirk/Spock, assuming that certain features of K/S, such as its 'utopian' aspects, characterize all slash. Since slash is based on the fictional worlds that the writers, directors and casts of many different television series have created, any given instance of slash necessarily possesses idiosyncratic features of the series from which it was derived. The reason that K/S has utopian aspects is that the original *Star Trek* series was animated by a utopian vision. Most television series that are 'slashed' do not share this vision and, therefore, neither does the slash that they inspire.

The most serious cost that academic slash theorists have incurred from being insufficiently comparative is their failure to situate slash within the context of women's romance fiction. In Chapter 6 we described the mainstream romance novel as a love story in the course of which the heroine overcomes obstacles to identify, win the heart of, and marry the one man who is right for her. With a few superficial changes in terminology (such as substituting 'form a permanent monogamous union with' for 'marry'), most students of slash would probably agree that this description also applies reasonably well to slash. But in a rush to show that slash, and by extension its fans, are 'different', academic theorists have seriously underestimated the similarities between slash and mainstream romances.

As indicated in the previous chapter, the following features have been identified by various theorists as being distinctive of slash: graphic descriptions of sexual activities; androgynous protagonists; shifting point of view/ multiple identifications; and egalitarian love relationships.

We argue below that, although these features do characterize slash, to a greater or lesser degree they also characterize women's erotic fiction in general.

Graphic descriptions of sexual activities

The average slash story is no doubt more sexually graphic than the average romance novel. But graphic sex is *not* an essential ingredient of *either* genre; one can find X, R and PG versions of both, and in some slash stories all the sex takes place 'off screen'. Although slash stories may include detailed descriptions of sexual acts, the emphasis is always on the emotional quality of the sex rather than on physical sensations, just as it is in mainstream romances. For example: ' "Touch me. Love me. Open me up for you. Then take me." Hutch swallowed, knowing that burning need and all his chaotic feelings were right on his face for Starsky to see' (*Just Another One of Starsky's Dirty Moves* by Flamingo).

In slash, as in mainstream romances, sex occurs within committed relationships as part of an emotionally mean-ingful exchange, and the story of developing love takes precedence over anatomical details. In mainstream romances and slash alike, sex serves the plot, whereas in male-oriented porn it is the other way around. Further-more, the artwork that illustrates many slash stories is unabashedly romantic and highly reminiscent of romance-novel cover art; it may portray nudity, but it almost never portrays penetration. Perhaps one reason why descriptions of sexual acts constitute a greater proportion of the average slash story than they do of the average romance novel is simply that a smaller proportion of slash needs to be devoted to character development and setting, since slash writers assume that their readers already possess this information.

Slash is often said to be more pornographic than other forms of women's erotica because it tends to contain more graphic sex, but in a sense it is actually *less* pornographic. The essence of male-oriented porn is not really the graphic depiction of sex (there is, after all, softcore porn), but, rather, the depiction of sex as an end in itself. No form of women's erotica depicts sex that way, but in the mainstream romance novel sexual attraction and, usually, sexual behaviour are integral to establishing the bond between hero and heroine. In slash, however, the bond of friendship is firmly in place long before sex rears its head.

Androgynous protagonists

Any appealing romance hero is likely to be an amalgam of traditionally masculine and feminine traits – if masculine traits include such things as being tall, reticent and sexually bold, and feminine traits include such things as being intuitive and a toucher. Recall Janice Radway's observation that the romance novel is an 'exercise in the imaginative transformation of masculinity to conform with female standards'.

Shifting point of view/multiple identifications

The heroine of a romance novel is its primary point-of-view character, but it is commonplace for the point of view to shift between heroine and hero, as many romance readers enjoy having a direct pipeline to the hero's feelings and thoughts. Similarly, although a shifting point of view is characteristic of slash, there is almost always a primary point-of-view character. What's more, this character is often portrayed as possessing some of the physical and psychological traits of a romance novel's heroine. In describing their protagonists' physical traits, writers of slash are to some extent constrained by the actual traits of the actors who play the parts; nevertheless, poetic licence frequently enables the main point-of-view character to be the smaller of the two, lighter in colouring, physically weaker, more seductive, more in touch with his emotions and quicker to perceive the existence of mutual love. Although both protagonists are ostensibly male, much is made of these physical and emotional differences. Napoleon Solo and Illya Kuryakin from *The Man from UNCLE* are good examples: 'Kuryakin's cool air of superiority and chilling competence often allowed Solo to forget how slight of stature his partner actually was, but in this incredibly intimate embrace, there was no disguising it' (*The Damage Control Affair* by Rosemary Callahan).

During an episode of anal sex in a slash story, each of the protagonists may play the role of both penetrator and penetratee, but the main point-of-view character plays the latter more frequently.

Egalitarian love relationships

The love relationships depicted in slash are undoubtedly 'egalitarian', which, as we have seen, does not mean that the protagonists are necessarily similar to each other; indeed, the men's strengths and weaknesses are often portrayed as complementary. But whether these relationships are *more* egalitarian than those depicted in mainstream romances is largely a matter of definition, of opinion and, let's face it, of sexual politics. After all, most readers and writers of mainstream romances would probably argue vehemently that the hero/heroine relationship is egalitarian. Despite the hero's much greater physical strength, he does not wield more power *within the couple's relationship* than the heroine does, and their dissimilar character traits, too, can be considered complementary.

And in slash, although battle-of-the-sexes themes are relatively muted, they are still present. As in mainstream romances, issues of commitment are explored ('Does he really love me?') and a naturally promiscuous masculine sexuality is transformed and harnessed by the power of love to create a permanent, intimate, nurturing, monogamous bond.

Other similarities between slash and mainstream romances

In academic analyses of the romance novel much is made of the heroine's giving her virginity to the hero. It is a common slash convention for one or both protagonists –

who have usually had a great deal of sexual experience with women – to be an 'anal virgin', which gives a whole new meaning to the phrase 'no one has ever made me feel this way before'. In both genres the loss of 'virginity' provides emotional resonance, affirming the couple's commitment to a bond they share with no one else. The prevalence and popularity in slash of 'first time' stories echoes the core theme of the romance novel: the search for the one right partner and the resolution of that search in sexual union.

The theme of exclusivity that permeates mainstream romances (as evidenced in possessiveness, jealousy and monogamy) is equally common in slash. The romance hero is very attractive and usually very sexually experienced, yet he loses interest in other women because the heroine is the only woman in the world who can make him happy. Similarly, Starsky tells Hutch, 'There's nobody else I want anymore . . . not since I realized that all the important feelings are between us . . . all the stuff that lasts a lifetime' (*April Fool's Day* by Candy Apple). In historical romances the entrance of a male rival often precipitates a duel, with the hero stating that he has come to claim what is his. In the *UNCLE* slash novel *City of Byzantium*, by Eros, Illya says to Napoleon: 'I don't mind if you look, I don't mind if you flirt. Both are as natural to you as breathing. But you unzip, and it's over.' New Age pundits and self-help gurus may claim that 'real' love is unpossessive, but, as cross-cultural and historical research by the anthropologist Helen Yonie Harris has conclusively documented, and as Darwinian theory would predict, one of the suite of features that, universally, constitutes the experience of romantic love is sexual jealousy.

Finally, the romance hero, according to Barlow and Krentz in *Dangerous Men and Adventurous Women*, is

a man in every sense of the word, and for most women the word man reverberates with thousands of years of connotative meanings, which touch upon everything from sexual prowess, capacity for honor/loyalty, to an ability to protect and defend the family unit. He is no weakling . . . he will be forced in the course of the plot to prove his commitment to the relationship.

This description also characterizes slash protagonists. They are men 'in every sense of the word' – cops, space explorers, secret agents, soldiers and so on – and each must prove that his love is strong enough to survive not only the plot twists typical of cop/spy/science-fiction stories, but also the conflicts that arise from the fact that he and his partner are (usually) heterosexual. These include internal conflict with the protagonist's own self-image as well as external conflict with friends, family, co-workers and an often homophobic world. It has been said that today, as in the past, the greatest adventure for the majority of women is finding a mate. In slash, the finding and accepting is the adventure. In sum, slash is so similar to mainstream romances that it can be regarded as a species of that genus. But there are, nonetheless, important differences. We shall now explain what we think makes slash distinctive and so appealing to its fans.

Why slash?

It is easy to think of reasons why a woman might prefer mainstream romances to slash: for example, she cannot suspend disbelief that two hetrosexual men would fall in love with one another; she can identify more easily with a female protagonist; she prefers to fantasize about a union that can produce children; she is uncomfortable with, or actually repelled by, the thought of sex between men; she prefers to identify with a protagonist who is a 'sex object' in the sense that her physical appearance arouses men's lust (slash protagonists aren't sex objects to each other in that sense).

If, as we have argued, slash and mainstream romances are in many ways very similar, why, given these good reasons to prefer the mainstream form, would anyone prefer slash? Our answers to this question are necessarily tentative and preliminary; hypotheses to be tested rather than firm conclusions. We will propose two kinds of hypothesis, which are mutually compatible. First, some women prefer the slash fantasy of being a co-warrior to the romance-novel fantasy of being a Mrs Warrior. Second, slash solves some of the dramatic problems inherent in the romance formula more successfully than mainstream romance literature can. By doing so, slash renders more plausible the obligatory happily-ever-after ending.

What's special about slash fans?

Our empirical research, described in the previous chapter, demonstrates that most romance readers, not just slash fans, can identify with one or both of the protagonists in a male/male love story and can enjoy reading such a story. Whatever it is that distinguishes slash fans from other romance readers, it almost certainly is *not* some sort of psychosexual oddity.

Slash fiction is based on friendship and shared adventure; its protagonists slay each others' dragons, both physical and emotional. Some women may prefer the fantasy of being a co-warrior to that of being a Mrs Warrior and the fantasy of being a hero who triumphs over the forces of evil to that of being a heroine who triumphs over an alpha male.

Who might such women be? Our research suggests at least one plausible, testable hypothesis. They might be, disproportionately, former tomboys who as adults enjoy buddy, action, science-fiction and horror movies: that is, women who are 'feminine' in their sexual psychology but somewhat 'masculine' in certain non-sexual respects. Research on tomboys has shown that most do not reject traditionally female activities, but rather, include traditionally male ones; for example, they may play with both dolls and toy trucks. During role-playing games they are more likely than non-tomboys to assume the male role. As adults, they typically score high on tests of assertiveness, competitiveness and willingness to take risks. Slash may have a special appeal to such women because it uniquely fuses traditionally female romance with traditionally male camaraderie, adventure and risk-taking.

Slash mitigates difficulties inherent in the romance formula

A problem faced by the romance writer is that to conclude her story successfully she (and her heroine) must vanquish male sexual psychology. This problem can be solved only to the extent that the reader is able and willing to suspend disbelief that such a triumph is possible. Shakespeare wrote of Cleopatra that 'Age cannot wither her, nor custom stale/Her infinite variety'; but 'other women cloy/The appetites they feed' and their charms presumably wither with age. For the perfect-union ending of a romance novel to be credible, the reader must believe that its heroine is another Cleopatra, and that in the years to come the hero will not be tempted by the opportunities that are bound to come the way of a high-mate-value 'warrior'. But, as the hero and heroine of a mainstream romance walk off into the sunset, how confident can we be that their perfect union will last?

Country-and-western star Randy Travis sang to his lover that if her hair turned grey, 'Baby, I wouldn't care/ I ain't in love with your hair.' Many women are sceptical of this kind of male assurance, and with good reason. A certain degree of female scepticism is what a Dawinian perspective should lead us to expect: intense sexual passion and romantic love are evanescent and, hence, a shaky foundation on which to build a long-term mateship. It would be surprising indeed if female mating adaptations did not incorporate in their designs such salient facts of life.

Slash mitigates this impediment to the happily-ever-after ending more successfully than mainstream romances can. Because the mutual fidelity of slash heroes has never been grounded in sexual passion for each other's bodies, it is far less vulnerable to the depredations of ages and the the temptation of new – especially younger – bodies. A slash protagonist need never wonder, 'Will he become bored with my body or love me less as my body withers with age?' because his partner's love didn't depend on physical appearance in the first place. In mainstream romances love originates in sexual passion, whereas in slash it originates in friendship; slash protagonists were comrades long before the scales fell from their eyes and they realized the existence of mutual love. In slash fiction a deep, abiding and *tested* friendship – developed in the complete absence of sexual attraction – is the rock-solid foundation upon which is erected the superstructure of romantic love, sexual passion and a permanent mateship.

This, we suspect, is the main reason why male/female slash is unlikely ever to replace male/male slash in the hearts of fans, even if many more television series come to feature opposite-sex pairings. With a male/female pairing, sexual tension (or, at least, mutual recognition of sexual possibilities) is ineluctably present from the outset, muddying the motivational waters and making it impossible to be certain whether the friendship would have been as strong in its absence. But slash protagonists put their hands in the fire for each other long before romantic love or sex were on the horizon.

Furthermore, slash almost 'automatically' solves a dramatic problem that is inherent in the romance formula. All romance fiction requires conflict – a barrier to keep the lovers temporarily apart. But the mainstream romance writer is in a bind. The more difficult the barrier is to surmount, the more intense the story and the stronger the protagonists' love must be to prevail; but the conflict must be capable of being resolved so completely that by the end of the story not a trace remains to mar the perfect union. A 'real' conflict – say, religious differences between hero and heroine – might well be resolved, perhaps by compromise, but it could not plausibly be resolved *completely*. Romance writers typically solve this problem by making the conflict trivial – often a misunderstanding so simple that if either of the protagonists had bothered to say 'What?!' there would have been no conflict. In slash, however, the conflict is inherent and compelling: two heterosexual men must overcome psychological and social barriers to recognize, accept and consummate their love. The barriers faced by slash protagonists are serious and inelucutable; and yet, together, the pair surmounts them. The happy ending of a slash story may thus be especially credible, since a love this strong can more plausibly be expected to last forever.

Happily ever after?

Helen Hazen, in her under-appreciated book *Endless Rapture*, argued that all women's fiction explores the same few themes: the problems inherent in finding, winning and retaining a suitable mate. Jane Austen represents the *haute cuisine* end of the continuum; genre romances represent the fast-food end. And just as the essential ingredients of universally popular fast food (sugar, salt and fat) provide clearer insight into evolved human gustatory adaptations than do the world's great cuisines (with all their complexities, idiosyncrasies and historical contingencies) so the essential ingredients of universally popular genre romances provide clearer insights into evolved female mating psychology than do the great works of fiction by women. For example, Jane Austen to the contrary notwithstanding, it is not *universally* acknowledged 'that a single man in possession of a good fortune, must be in want of a wife'. For one thing, throughout the overwhelming majority of human evolutionary history there was no such thing as 'a good fortune'. The essential ingredients of romances – mainstream and slash alike – imply that a truth *more* universally acknowledged is that a single, tall, strong, handsome, healthy, intelligent, confident, physically and socially competent 'warrior' must be in want of a mate.

Perhaps the main lesson to be learned from slash is the rather banal one that the more things appear to change in the domain of human mating psychology the more they actually remain the same. Bizarre as slash stories may seem at first blush, they are really about achieving the perfect mateship, just as mainstream romances are. This lesson may seem a bit less banal when viewed against the background of erotic genres that women could be producing and consuming but aren't. For example, women could easily create and disseminate via the internet a genre of erotic fiction in which a female point-of-view character has impersonal sex with an endless succession of high-mate-value men without ever forming – or seeking to form – a durable relationship with any of them. But, to our knowledge, no such genre exists. In sum, most of the features of human female mating psychology that can be inferred from an analysis of mainstream women's erotica can also be inferred from our analysis of slash. Indeed, we have argued that building a romantic/sexual relationship on the solid foundation of an established friendship, which is the core theme of slash, actually achieves some of the goals of mainstream romances more successfully than do these romances themselves.

In his essay 'On Friendship', Montaigne wrote, perhaps a bit wistfully, of male/male friendship that 'if such a relationship, free and voluntary, could be built up, in which not only would the souls have this complete enjoyment, but the bodies would also share in the alliance, so that the entire man would be engaged, it is certain that the resulting friendship would be fuller and more complete'. For better or for worse, this can't happen to heterosexual men. But it happens all the time, in the realm of the imagination, to the many women who read and write slash fiction.

ACKNOWLEDGEMENTS

We thank Donald Brown, Peter Tallack, and the series editors, Helena Cronin and Oliver Curry, for their very helpful comments on the entire manuscript. We also thank Edward Hagen and Nicole Hess for their expert guidance on Chapters 2 and 3.

SUGGESTIONS FOR FURTHER READING

••

Daly, Martin and Wilson, Margo, *The Truth About Cinderella: A Darwinian View of Parental Love*, London: Weidenfeld & Nicolson (1998).

Lamb, Patricia Fraser and Veith, Dianna L., 'Romantic Myth, Transcendence, and *Star Trek* Zines', in D. Palumbo (ed.) *Erotic Universe: Sexuality and Fantastic Literature*, New York: Greenwood Press (1986).

Geary, David, *Male, Female: The Evolution of Human Sex Differences*, Washington, DC: American Psychological Association (1998).

Hazen, Helen, *Endless Rapture: Rape, Romance, and the Female Imagination*, New York: Charles Scribner's Sons (1983).

Jenkins, Henry, *Textual Poachers: Television Fans and Participatory Culture*, New York: Routledge (1992).

Krentz, Jayne Ann (ed.), *Dangerous Men and Adventurous Women*, Philadelphia, Pa.: University of Pennsylvania Press (1992).

Penley, Constance and Ross, A. (eds), *Technoculture*, Minneapolis: University of Minnesota Press (1991).

Russ, Joanna, 'Pornography for women, by women,

with love', in *Magic Mommas, Trembling Sisters, Puritans and Perverts: Feminist Essays*, Trumansburg, NY: The Crossing Press (1985).

Symons, Donald, *The Evolution of Human Sexuality*, New York: Oxford University Press (1979).